IT'S IN THE BAG
KNITTING PROJECTS TO TAKE & MAKE

EDITED BY KARA GOTT WARNER

HOUSE of
WHITE
BIRCHES

PUBLISHERS
SINCE 1947

IT'S IN THE BAG™

EDITOR Kara Gott Warner
ART DIRECTOR Brad Snow
PUBLISHING SERVICES DIRECTOR Brenda Gallmeyer

MANAGING EDITOR Dianne Schmidt
ASSISTANT ART DIRECTOR Nick Pierce
COPY SUPERVISOR Michelle Beck
COPY EDITORS Amanda Ladig, Susanna Tobias
TECHNICAL EDITOR Charlotte Quiggle
TECHNICAL ARTISTS Nicole Gage, Pam Gregory

GRAPHIC ARTS SUPERVISOR Ronda Bechinski
GRAPHIC ARTISTS Jessi Butler, Minette Collins Smith
PRODUCTION ASSISTANTS Marj Morgan, Judy Neuenschwander

PHOTOGRAPHY SUPERVISOR Tammy Christian
PHOTOGRAPHY Scott Campbell, Matthew Owen
PHOTO STYLISTS Martha Coquat, Tammy Steiner

PRINTED IN CHINA
FIRST PRINTING: 2009
LIBRARY OF CONGRESS CONTROL NUMBER: 2008936680
HARDCOVER ISBN: 978-1-59217-247-4
SOFTCOVER ISBN: 978-1-59217-248-1

1 2 3 4 5 6 7 8 9
DRGbooks.com

WELCOME

The concept of this book is one that is near and dear to my heart. As a knitter, it's imperative to have just the right bag, equipped with a fun project and all the important essentials. The "travel-friendly" projects that follow will entice you to pack up your favorite knitting bag (or even buy a new one) and head out the door at a moment's notice. In addition to the range of projects to choose from, we also provide some valuable

travel tips and tricks. Whether you choose to knit with friends, or in solitude, you'll always have your favorite "friend" nearby.

Our designers also share some of their own memorable stories about traveling with their knitting in tow. My story begins back in the time when I commuted by subway each morning to midtown Manhattan. Finding a seat on the subway was virtually impossible during a busy morning commute. Since standing was usually the only option, I was determined to always make the most of it! My yarn was set in such a way that it would flow out of my bag tangle-free, with my instructions positioned in just the right place. When thinking back to the stares of curiosity, I'm sure I provided the subway riders with some much needed entertainment.

I'll never forget the last day of my regular commute downtown, which is a day that I fondly think back to with a smile. I knew then that I would miss this special time each morning dedicated to my knitting. While some may think of being on the subway as a nuisance, I always viewed it as an opportunity. As it became time to get off at my usual stop, a young woman asked me, "How did you do that?" As we proceeded up the steps, I gave her the "quickie" version of how to work a particular stitch. We said good-bye and off we went on our separate ways down the busy city street.

Wishing you memorable knitting adventures!

Kara Gott Warner

Kara Gott Warner

CONTENTS

ACCENT ACCESSORIES

Just as the party starts to die down, spice things up and knit a round or two. In this chapter, you'll love the selection of projects that will be a breeze to make while you travel! Pack that favorite knitting purse, grab some yummy yarn, and let's party!

UPTOWN CHIC SATCHEL

DESIGN BY CECILY GLOWIK MACDONALD

WHAT'S IN THE BAG

Classic Elite Yarns Duchess (bulky weight; 40% merino/28% viscose/15% nylon/10% cashmere/7% angora; 75 yds/ 50g per ball): 4 balls genteel gray #1003

Size 9 (5.5mm) needles or size needed to obtain gauge

Stitch markers

Cable needle

2 handles with 12-inch opening (sample made with Trendsetter yarns BH-MED/B, 12-inch length)

Cardboard (optional)

SKILL LEVEL

 INTERMEDIATE

FINISHED SIZE

12 inches wide x 7 inches tall

GAUGE

16 sts and 20 rows = 4 inches/10cm in St st.

To save time, take time to check gauge.

SPECIAL ABBREVIATION

Make Bobble (MB): Knit in front and back of st, turn; p3, turn, k3, turn; p3, turn; SK2P.

PATTERN STITCHES

Front/Back Panel pat: See Chart A
Side Panel pat: See Chart B.

Slip Stitch Pattern (multiple of 2 sts + 1)
Rows 1 and 3 (WS): Purl.
Row 2 (RS): *K1, sl 1; rep from * to last st, k1.
Row 4: K1, *k1, sl 1; rep from * to last 2 sts, k2.

   Rep Rows 1–4 for pat.

FRONT/BACK PIECES

Make 2

Cast on 51 sts.

Row 1 (WS): P17, place marker, work 17 sts following Chart A, place marker, k17.

   Continue working outer sts in St st and sts between markers following Chart A until 1 full rep of chart has been worked, then work Rows 1–9 of Chart A once more.

Next row: Work as for Row 10 of chart except do not work bobble; purl the st instead.

Next row (WS): P16, p2tog, p15, p2tog, p16—49 sts.

   Work 4 rows in St st.

   Bind off kwise.

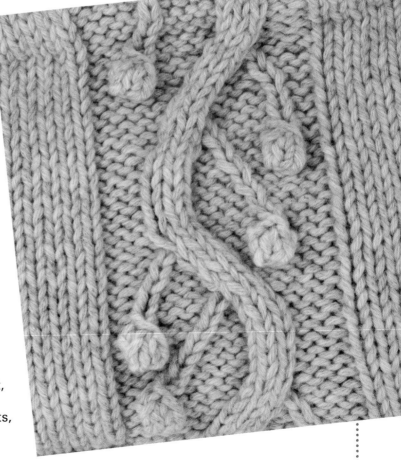

SIDE PIECES
Make 2
Cast on 23 sts.
  Work Chart B.
  Bind off pwise.

BOTTOM
Cast on 23 sts.
  Work even in
Slip Stitch pat until
piece measures 12
inches, ending with
a RS row.
  Bind off pwise.

FINISHING
Block pieces.
  Sew cast-on edge of 1 front/back piece to
1 long edge of bottom. Rep with other front/
back piece. Sew cast-on edges of side pieces
to short edges of bottom. Sew side seams
leaving 1 inch unsewn at top of all pieces. Slide
bound-off edge of 1 front/back piece through
slit in handle. Wrap around bottom of handle
and sew bound-off edge of front/back piece
to inside of bag; rep for 2nd handle. Fold top 1
inch of side panels to WS and sew to inside of
bag. Weave in ends.
  Optional: For a sturdier bottom, cut a piece
of cardboard to measurements slightly smaller
than bottom piece and place inside bag. ■

STITCH KEY
- ☐ K on RS, p on WS
- ⊟ P on RS, k on WS
- ⊠ Ssp
- ⊠ P2tog
- ⊙ MB: Knit in front and back of st, turn; p3, turn; k3, turn; p3, turn; SK2P
- ⟋ Sl 2 to cn and hold in back, k3, p2 from cn
- ⟍ Sl 3 to cn and hold in front, p2, k3 from cn
- ⟋ Sl 1 to cn and hold in back, k1, p1 from cn
- ⟍ Sl 1 to cn and hold in front, p1, k1 from cn

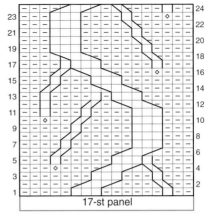

17-st panel

CHART A: FRONT/BACK PANEL

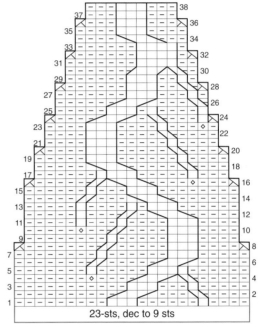

23-sts, dec to 9 sts

CHART B: SIDE PANEL

Tip   If you have several projects going at one time, keep a mini "travel filing cabinet." These come in many fun shapes and sizes. You can keep track of your supplies, who you made your project for and where you last left off.

LITTLE MISS HAT & PURSE

DESIGNS BY CHERYL BECKERICH

WHAT'S IN THE BAG

Schaefer Yarn Elaine (bulky weight; 99% merino wool/1% nylon; 300 yds/8 oz per skein): 1 skein Peter (A)

Plymouth Galway Worsted (worsted weight; 100% wool, 210 yds/100g per ball): 1 ball rose #114 (B)

Size 9 (5.5mm) double-point needle (set of 4 or 5) and 16-inch circular needles or size needed to obtain gauge

Stitch markers, 1 in CC for beg of rnd

SKILL LEVEL

 EASY

SIZES

Bag: 1 size

Hat: Child's small (medium, large) Instructions are given for smallest size, with larger sizes in parentheses. When only 1 number is given, it applies to all sizes.

FINISHED MEASUREMENTS

Bag: 7 inches wide at base; 6 inches wide at top; 6 inches high

Hat circumference (body): 17 (18, 19) inches

GAUGE

20 sts and 21 rows = 4 inches/10cm in Slip St Mesh with MC.

14½ sts and 20 rows = 4 inches/10cm in seed st with MC.

To save time, take time to check gauge.

SPECIAL ABBREVIATIONS

Place marker (pm): Place a marker on the needle.

Increase 1 (inc 1): Knit in front and back of st.

PATTERN STITCHES

Slip Stitch Mesh (even number of sts)

Rnds 1 and 2: Purl.

Rnd 3: *Sl 1, k1; rep from * around.

Rnd 4: *Sl 1, p1; rep from * around.

Rnd 5: *Yo, k2tog; rep from * around.

Rnd 6: Knit.

Rep Rnds 1–6 for pat.

Seed Stitch (odd number of sts)

Rnd/Row 1: K1, *p1, k1; rep from * to end.

Rnd/Row 2: Knit the purl sts and purl the knit sts as they present themselves.

Rep Rnd/Row 2 for pat.

SPECIAL TECHNIQUE

3-Needle Bind-Off: With RS tog and needles parallel, using a 3rd needle, knit tog 1 st from the front needle with 1 from the back. *Knit tog 1 st from the front and back needles, and sl the first st over the 2nd to bind off. Rep from * across, then fasten off last st.

BAG

BASE

With A, cast on 9 sts.

Work in Seed st until piece measures 7¼ inches.

Bind off, do not cut yarn.

BODY

Pick up and knit 7 sts along bound-off end, pm, pick up and knit 28 sts along side, pm, pick up and knit 7 sts from cast-on end, pm, pick up and knit 28 sts along rem side, pm for beg of rnd and join—70 sts.

Set-up rnd: Slipping markers, *work in seed st to first marker, work in Slip St Mesh to next marker; rep from * once more.

Continue in established pats until 2 reps of Slip St Mesh are complete.

Dec rnd: Continue in established pats, *work to first marker, p1, p2tog, work in pat to 3 sts before next marker, p2tog, p1; rep from * once more—66 sts.

Work even in established pat for 5 rnds.

Rep Dec rnd—62 sts.

Work even for 16 rnds, ending with Rnd 5 of pat.

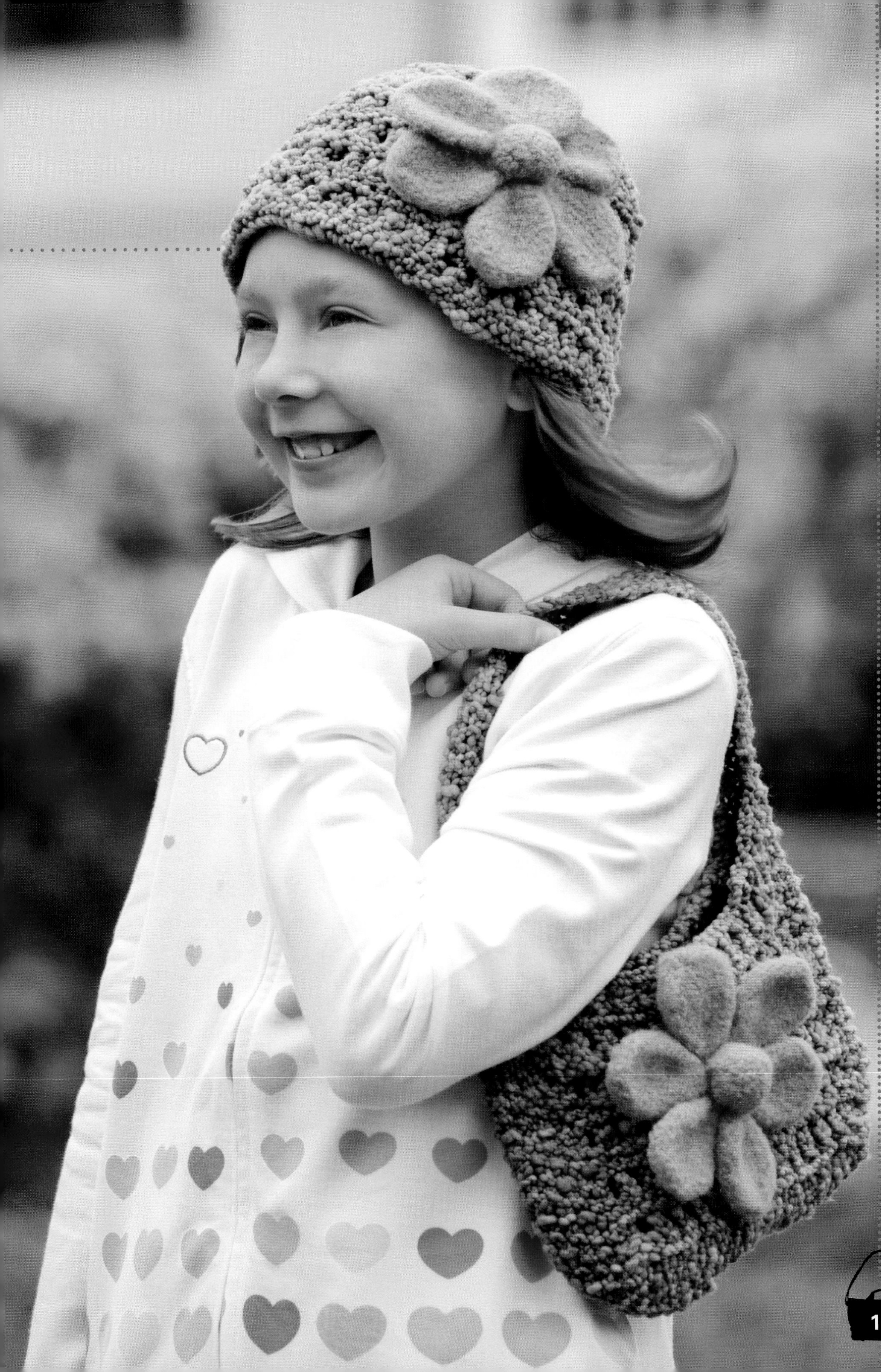

Next rnd: Removing markers, *work in Seed st to marker, k5, bind off 14 sts, knit to next marker; rep from * once more, then work Seed st to first bind-off.

Slip 17 sts at other end to holder—17 sts rem on needle.

HANDLES
Working all sts in established Seed st, bind off 3 sts at beg of next 2 rows; bind off 2 sts at beg of following 2 rows; then bind off 1 st at beg of following 2 rows—5 sts.

Work even until handle measures 6 inches and put sts on holder.

Rep for the other side.

Join the 2 ends of the handle with 3-Needle Bind-Off.

FINISHING
Weave in ends and block.

HAT

BRIM
With circular needles and A, and using long tail method, cast on 90 (96, 100) sts; pm for beg of rnd and join, taking care not to twist sts.

Work 5 rnds in Slip St Mesh.
Dec rnd: Work Rnd 6 of pat and dec 10 sts evenly around—80 (86, 90) sts.

Continue in Slip St Mesh for 5 rnds.
Dec rnd: Work Rnd 6 of pat and dec 20 sts evenly around—60 (66, 70) sts.

BODY
Work [Rnds 1–6 of Slip Stitch Mesh pat] 4 times.

Purl 0 (1, 2) rnds.

Shape crown
Work Rnd 1 of Slip St Mesh.
Dec rnd: Work Rnd 2 of pat and dec 20 sts evenly around—40 (46, 50) sts.

Work Rnds 3–6 of pat.
Dec rnd: Work Rnd 1 of pat and dec 10 (12, 10) sts evenly around—30 (34, 40) sts.

Work Rnds 2-5 of pat.
Dec rnd: [K2tog] around—15 (17, 20) sts.
Dec rnd: [P2tog] around, ending p1 (1, 0)—8 (9, 10) sts.

Cut yarn, leaving a 6-inch tail.

With tapestry needle, thread tail through rem sts, pull tight and secure.

FINISHING
Weave in tails. Block.

FELTED FLOWERS
Make 2

Center
With dpn and B, cast on 6 sts; distribute sts evenly on 3 dpns, pm for beg of rnd and join, taking care not to twist sts.
Rnd 1: Knit.
Rnd 2: Inc 1 in each st around—12 sts.
Rnd 3: Knit.
Rnd 4: *K1, inc 1; rep from * around—18 sts.
Rnd 5: Knit.
Rnd 6: *K2, inc 1; rep from * around—24 sts.
Cut yarn.

Petals
Make 6 on each flower
Distribute sts among the dpns so that you

have 4 sts on 1 dpn and 20 rem sts on hold on 2 dpns to be worked later.

Row 1 (WS): P4.

Inc row: K1, inc 1, work to last 2 sts, inc 1, k1—6 sts.

Continue in St st and rep Inc row [every RS row] twice more—10 sts.

Work 7 rows even.

Next row (RS): K1, ssk, k4, k2tog, k1—8 sts.

Next row (WS): P1, p2tog, p2, ssp, p1—6 sts.

Next row: K1, ssk, k2tog, k1—4 sts.

Next row: P2tog, ssp—2 sts.

Bind off.

Rep for each petal.

SHAPING

With tapestry needle and approx 10 inches of yarn, weave the yarn in and out around the base of the petals to form a bobble in center of flower and place tails in the center of the flower as stuffing for the bobble. Pull tight and secure yarn.

Weave in rem tails.

FELTING

Follow basic felting instructions on page 167 until flowers measure approx 5½ inches across.

ASSEMBLY

Sew flowers to bag and hat, being careful to catch only the back of the petals and center of flowers so that yarn doesn't show on the RS. ■

Tip Place a copy of your pattern in a page protector. Use a dry erase marker to remember your place. When you're done, just wipe it clean.

KATHMANDU CRAVAT

DESIGN BY JOËLLE MEIER RIOUX FOR CLASSIC ELITE YARNS

WHAT'S IN THE BAG

Classic Elite Yarns Fresco (sport weight; 60% wool/30% baby alpaca/10% angora; 164 yds/50g per hank): 1 hank each purple haze #5379 (A) and cinder #5303 (B)
Size 7 (4.5mm) needles or size needed to obtain gauge

2 FINE

SKILL LEVEL

 BEGINNER

FINISHED SIZE

Approx 4 x 30 inches

GAUGE

33 sts and 26 rows = 4 inches/10cm in Biased Rib.
To save time, take time to check gauge.

SPECIAL ABBREVIATIONS

Make 1 (M1): Insert LH needle from front to back under the running thread between the last st worked and next st on RH needle; knit into the back of resulting loop.
Make 1 purlwise (M1P): Insert LH needle from front to back under the running thread between the last st worked and next st on RH needle; purl into the back of resulting loop.

PATTERN STITCHES

K3, P3 Rib (multiple of 6 sts +3)
Row 1 (RS): K3, *p3, k3; rep from * across.
Row 2: Knit the knit sts and purl the purl sts as they face you.
    Rep Row 2 for pat.

Biased Rib (multiple of 6 sts + 3)
Rows 1, 5 and 9 (RS): K3, M1P, knit the knit sts and purl the purl sts as they face you to last 4 sts, k2tog, k2.
Rows 2, 3, 4, 6, 7, 8, 10, 11, 12, 14, 15, 16, 18, 19, 20, 22, 23 and 24: K3, knit the knit sts and purl the purl sts as they face you to last 3 sts, k3.

Rows 13, 17 and 21: K3, M1, knit the knit sts and purl the purl sts as they face you to last 4 sts, k2tog, k2.
    Rep Rows 1–24 for pat.

Stripe Sequence
*Work 33 rows with A, then 33 rows with B; rep from * twice more.

PATTERN NOTE

First and last 3 stitches are worked in garter stitch (knit every row) throughout.

SCARF

With A, cast on 33 sts.
Row 1 (RS): Beg Stripe Sequence; k3, work K3, P3 Rib to last 3 sts, k3.
    Maintaining first and last 3 sts in garter st throughout, work even for 5 rows in established rib, ending with a WS row.
Next row (RS): Continue Stripe sequence and change to Biased Rib.
    Work even until Stripe Sequence is complete, ending with Row 24 of Biased Rib.
    Bind off in pat.

FINISHING

Weave in all ends. Block to finished measurements. ∎

Tip If your project calls for straight needles, try circulars instead. You can work the same as you would on straight needles, and you won't have to fumble around to find the straight needle that fell into the "black hole" of your knitting bag ever again!

DAY AT THE MET MITERED WRAP

DESIGN BY SARA LUCAS

WHAT'S IN THE BAG

Plymouth Boku (worsted weight; 95% wool/5% silk; 99 yds/50g per ball): 2 balls blue-green variegated #10 (A)

Berroco Comfort (worsted weight; 50% nylon/50% acrylic; 210 yds/100g per ball): 1 ball each dried plum #9780 (B), barley #9703 (C) and limone #9706 (D)

Size 8 (5mm) needles or size needed to obtain gauge

SKILL LEVEL

◼◼◼◻ INTERMEDIATE

FINISHED MEASUREMENTS

Approx 18 x 56 inches

GAUGE

18 sts and 36 rows = 4 inches/10cm in garter st. To save time, take time to check gauge.

SPECIAL ABBREVIATION

Centered Double Decrease (S2KP2): Slip 2 sts kwise, k1, pass 2 slipped sts over.

PATTERN STITCHES

Color Sequence
Work 3 rows A, 2 rows B, 2 rows A, 2 rows C, 2 rows A, 2 rows D, 8 rows A, work B to end.

Mitered Square

With A, cast on or pick up and knit a total of 30 sts.

Row 1 (WS): K14, k2tog, k14—29 sts.
Row 2 (RS): K13, S2KP2, k13—27 sts.
Row 3 and all WS rows: Knit.
Row 4: K12, S2KP2, k12—25 sts.
Row 6: K11, S2KP2, k11—23 sts.

Continue in this manner, working garter st with centered double dec at center st every RS row until 3 sts rem.

Next row (WS): Work S2KP2 and fasten off.

Mitered Rectangle

With A, cast on or pick up and knit a total of 60 sts.

Row 1 (WS): K14, k2tog, k28, k2tog, k14—58 sts.
Row 2 (RS): K13, S2KP2, k26, S2KP2, k13—54 sts
Row 3 and all other WS rows: Knit.
Row 4: K12, S2KP2, k24, S2KP2, k12—50 sts.

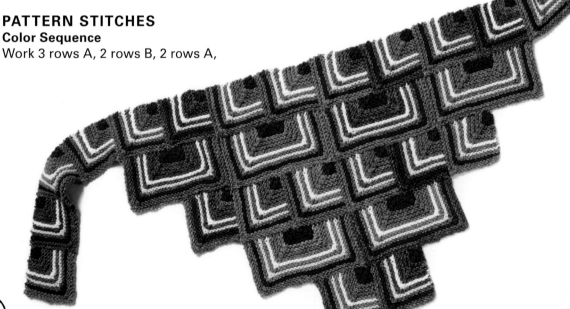

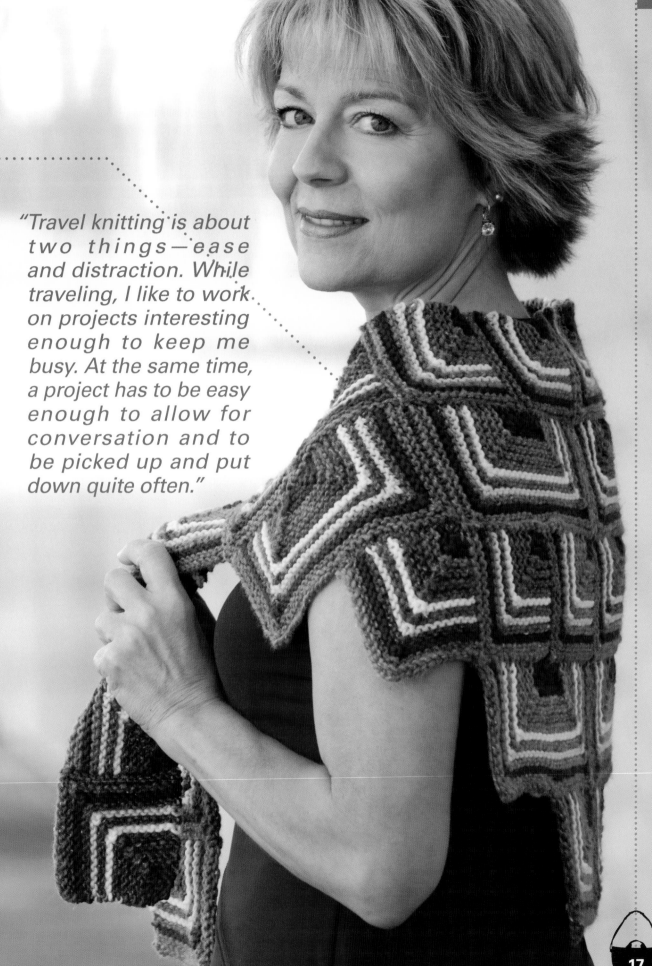

"Travel knitting is about two things—ease and distraction. While traveling, I like to work on projects interesting enough to keep me busy. At the same time, a project has to be easy enough to allow for conversation and to be picked up and put down quite often."

Row 6: K11, S2KP2, k22, S2KP2, k11—46 sts.

Continue in this manner, working garter st with centered double dec every RS row until 2 sts rem.

Next row (WS): K2tog and fasten off.

PATTERN NOTES

Wrap is worked from bottom up with mitered squares and rectangles (see Placement Diagram for order).

Use knit-on method when casting on.

When picking up stitches pick up 1 stitch per stitch or garter ridge.

Use color A to begin each square or rectangle, then follow Color Sequence.

The beginning sides (cast-on or pick-up) of squares are Side A and Side B; the beginning sides of rectangles are Sides A, B, and C (see Diagram).

Weave in ends as you work to avoid excess finishing.

WRAP

Square 1: With A, cast on 30 sts. Work Mitered Square following Color Sequence.

Square 2: With A, pick up and knit 15 sts along Side C of Square 1, then cast on 15 sts—30 sts. Work Mitered Square.

Rectangle 3: Cast on 30 sts, pick up and knit 15 sts along Side D of Square 1, then cast on 15 sts—60 sts. Work Mitered Rectangle.

Rectangle 4: Pick up and knit 15 sts along Side C of Rectangle 3, then 15 sts along Side D of Square 2, cast on 30 sts—60 sts. Work Mitered Rectangle.

Square 5: Cast on 30 sts. Work Mitered Square.

Square 6: Pick up and knit 15 sts along Side C of Square 5, and 15 sts along Side D of Rectangle 3—30 sts. Work Mitered Square.

Continue in this manner, working each square or rectangle in order following Diagram, casting on or picking up as appropriate.

FINISHING

Weave in all rem ends and block. ∎

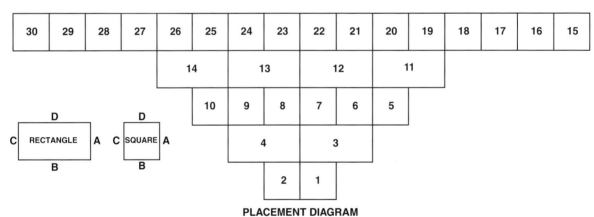

PLACEMENT DIAGRAM

COUNTRY ROADS SCARF

DESIGN BY KYLEANN WILLIAMS

WHAT'S IN THE BAG

Crystal Palace Merino 5 (worsted weight; 100% superwash wool; 110 yds/50g per ball): 3 balls each fall herbs #9809 (A) and nougat #5216 (B)
Size 10 (6mm) needles or size needed to obtain gauge

SKILL LEVEL

■■□□ EASY

FINISHED SIZE

Approx 10 x 66 inches (blocked)

GAUGE

17 sts and 23 rows = 4 inches/10cm in St st.
To save time, take time to check gauge.

SPECIAL ABBREVIATION

Make 1 (M1): Insert LH needle from front to back under the running thread between the last st worked and next st on RH needle; knit into the back of resulting loop.

PATTERN NOTES

This scarf is worked in entrelac. "Steps" are spelled out, rather than "Rows;" most steps are worked across and then back, i.e. 2 rows in most steps.

The body of the scarf is made in stockinette stitch; the sides and ends are made in seed stitch to eliminate curling and minimize blocking.

Always work the stitches in the row following the pick-up row through the back loop; this will twist the base of the picked-up stitch, keeping that loop from being too loose.

SCARF

Foundation Triangles
Make 3

With A, very loosely cast on 21 sts, using a larger needle if necessary.
Step 1: K1, p1, turn; p1, k1, turn.
Step 2: K1, p1, k1, turn; k1, p1, k1, turn.
Step 3: [K1, p1] twice, turn; [p1, k1] twice, turn.
Step 4: K1, [p1, k1] twice, turn; k1, [p1, k1] twice, turn.
Step 5: [K1, p1] 3 times, turn; [p1, k1] 3 times, turn.
Step 6: K1, [p1, k1] 3 times, do not turn—7 sts worked.

Rep [Steps 1–6] twice more over the last 14 sts.

Cut A, leaving a 5-inch tail.

FIRST TIER

Left Side Triangle
Step 1 (WS): Join B; k1, p1, turn; p1, M1, p1, turn.
Step 2: P1, k1, p2tog, turn; p1, k1, M1, k1, turn.
Step 3: K1, p1, k1, p2tog, turn; p1, k1, p1, M1, p1, turn.
Step 4: [P1, k1] twice, p2tog; turn [p1, k1] twice, M1, k1, turn.
Step 5: [K1, p1] twice, k1, p2tog; turn, [p1, k1] twice, p1, M1, p1, turn.
Step 6: [P1, k1] 3 times, p2tog; do not turn.

Right Slanting Rectangle

Step 1 (WS): Pick up and purl 7 sts along the selvedge edge of triangle or rectangle of tier below, turn.

Step 2: K7, turn; p6, p2tog, turn.

Rep [Step 2] 6 more times; do not turn after last p2tog—rectangle complete.

Work another Right Slanting Rectangle over the next 7 sts.

Right Side Triangle

Step 1 (WS): Pick up and purl 7 sts along the selvedge edge of the next triangle or rectangle, turn.

Step 2: [K1, p1] 3 times, k1 turn; [k1, p1] 2 twice, k1, k2tog, turn.

Step 3: [P1, k1] 3 times, turn; [k1, p1] twice, k2tog, turn.

Step 4: [K1, p1] twice, k1, turn; k1, p1, k1, k2tog, turn.

Step 5: [P1, k1] twice, turn; k1, p1, k2tog, turn.

Step 6: K1, p1, k1, turn; k1, k2tog, turn.

Step 7: P1, k1, turn; k2tog, turn—1 st rem.

Cut B, leaving a 5-inch tail.

2ND TIER

Left Slanting Rectangle

Step 1 (RS): With A, pick up and knit 6 sts along edge of triangle just completed, turn—7 sts, including last st from right side triangle.

Step 2: P7, turn; k6, ssk.

Rep [Step 2] 6 more times.

Make 2 more Left Slanting Rectangles, picking up 7 sts along the edges of the Right Slanting Rectangles in the tier below.

Cut A, leaving a 5-inch tail.

"Circular needles really come in handy when knitting on a plane. You're not a true knitter if you've never dropped a straight needle, and watched it roll all the way to the cockpit"!

Work 25 more reps of first and 2nd tiers, ending with first tier.

ENDING TRIANGLES

Make 3

Step 1: With A, pick up and knit 6 sts along side of triangle just completed, turn—7 sts, including last st from Right Side Triangle.

Step 2: K1, [p1, k1] 3 times, turn; [k1, p1] 3 times, ssk, turn.

Step 3: [K1, p1] twice, k1, p2tog, turn; p1, [k1, p1] twice, ssk, turn.

Step 4: [K1, p1] twice, k2tog, turn; [k1, p1] twice, ssk, turn.

Step 5: K1, p1, k1, p2tog, turn; p1, k1, p1, ssk, turn.

Step 6: K1, p1, k2tog, turn; k1, p1, ssk, turn.

Step 7: K1, p2tog, turn, p1, ssk, turn.

Step 8: K2tog, turn; ssk, do not turn.

Rep [Steps 1–8] twice more, picking up sts along sides of rectangles of previous tier.

Fasten off.

FINISHING

Weave in ends. Wet-block the scarf and let dry thoroughly. ∎

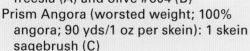

SIMPLY STRIPES SCARF

DESIGN BY LAURA BRYANT FOR PRISM YARN

WHAT'S IN THE BAG

Prism Lotus (worsted
   weight; 58% wool/27%
   bamboo/15% silk; 105 yds/2
   oz per skein): 1 skein each
   freesia (A) and olive #604 (B)
Prism Angora (worsted weight; 100%
   angora; 90 yds/1 oz per skein): 1 skein
   sagebrush (C)
Size 10 (6mm) 29-inch circular needle or
   size needed to obtain gauge
Size 13 (9mm) 29-inch circular needle
Cardboard, 8-inches wide

4 MEDIUM

SKILL LEVEL
■□□□ BEGINNER

FINISHED SIZE
Approx 6 x 57 inches, not including fringe

GAUGE
14 sts and 28 rows = 4 inches/10cm in
garter stitch with smaller needle. To
save time, take time to check gauge.

PATTERN NOTES
This scarf is knit sideways and is self-
fringing.

   Leave an 8-inch tail when attaching or
cutting each yarn; when turning between
first and 2nd row of each color, wrap yarn
around an 8-inch piece of cardboard,
then continue with 2nd row.

Tip   "Fringe as you work" is the perfect
solution for working with multiple
yarns. When you finish a row, cut
the yarn and turn it into fringe. You
can be resourceful and use your paperback
book to conveniently measure it too!

SCARF

With A and larger needle, cast on 200 sts.
   With smaller needle, work in garter stitch,
leaving 8-inch lengths for fringe at each end
of row *(see Pattern Notes)*, in the following
sequence: 2 rows A, 2 rows B, 2 rows C.
   Work for 6 inches (or desired width),
finishing with A or B.
   Bind off with larger needle.
   Make an overhand knot at edge of fabric
with every 2–3 strands of yarn.
   Cut fringe evenly. ■

CITY GIRL SCARF

DESIGN BY JACQUELINE W. HOYLE

WHAT'S IN THE BAG

Schaefer Yarn Judith (DK weight;
   100% prime alpaca; 330 yds/4oz
   per skein): 1 skein Renata
   Tebaldi

Size 10 (6mm) needles or size needed to
   obtain gauge

SKILL LEVEL

 EASY

FINISHED SIZE

Approx 4 x 68 inches, not including fringes

GAUGE

17 sts and 32 rows = 4 inches/10cm in Lacy pat.
To save time, take time to check gauge.

PATTERN STITCH

Lacy Pattern (any number of sts)
Row 1: K1, *[yo] twice, k1; rep from * to end.

Row 2: K1, *drop both yo's, k1; rep from *
to end.
Rows 3–10: Knit.
   Rep Rows 1–10 for pat.

PATTERN NOTE

When casting on at the beginning of a row to
start a fringe, turn work and use cable cast-
on method, then turn work again and work
stitches following instructions.

SCARF

Cast on 18 sts.
   Knit 6 rows.

First Fringe Section

Rows 1 and 2 (side fringes): Cast on 18 sts,
turn; k18, turn; p18, turn; bind
off the 18 cast on sts, then k18 rem sts.
Row 3: K1, *yo, k1; rep from *
to end.
Row 4: K1, *drop yo, k1; rep from * to end.
Rows 5 and 6: Knit.
Rows 7 and 8: Rep Rows 1 and 2.
Rows 9–11: Knit.
   Rep [Rows 1–11] 8 times.

Main Section

Work Lacy pat until scarf is desired length
minus the length of fringe section.

Second Fringe section

Work Rows 3–11 of first fringe section, then
work [Rows 1–11] 8 times, and [Rows 1 and 2]
once.
   Knit 6 rows.
   Bind off loosely.
   Weave in all ends. ■

Tip Place your yarn into a resealable
plastic bag. Cut a small hole in the
bottom corner and pull the end of
the yarn through the opening.

KALEIDOSCOPE MARKET BAG

DESIGN BY CELESTE PINHEIRO

WHAT'S IN THE BAG

Plymouth Galway Worsted (worsted weight; 100% wool; 210 yds/100g per ball): 1 ball each dark brown #66 (A), mulberry #117 (B), lime #127 (C), orange #91 (D), pink #141 (E), turquoise #149 (F), light purple #89 (G) and gold #60 (H)

Size 8 (5mm) straight and 24-inch circular needles or size needed to obtain gauge

Open stitch marker

½ yd of fabric (optional for lining)

SKILL LEVEL

■■■☐ INTERMEDIATE

FINISHED MEASUREMENTS

Length: 14 inches
Width: 13½ inches

GAUGE

18 sts and 23 rows=4 inches in St st.
To save time, take time to check gauge.

PATTERN NOTES

Bag is worked from bottom up.

The mitered squares are worked in 2 color sequences: A and B.

The instructions for Square A are given first; instructions for Square B are in parentheses.

Place center stitch marker in the fabric, not on the needle; the center stitch will become obvious after you've worked several decrease rows but if necessary move marker up as you work.

Weave in ends as you work to eliminate tedious finishing.

Refer to Figure 1 for labeled points and sides.

Refer to Figure 2 for placement of Squares A and B when working bag.

BAG

SQUARE A (B)

With B (G) cast on 39 sts and mark center st.
Knit 1 WS row.

Row 1 (RS): Knit to 1 st before center st, sk2p, knit to end—37 sts.

Continuing to work sk2p dec over center 3 sts every RS row and purling all sts on WS rows through Row 28, work as follows:

Row 2: Purl.
Row 3: Knit—35 sts.
Row 4: Purl.
Row 5: Knit—33 sts.
Row 6: Change to A (A) and knit.
Row 7: Knit—31 sts.
Row 8: Purl.
Row 9: Knit—29 sts.
Row 10: Change to C (H) and knit.
Row 11: Knit—27 sts.
Row 12: Purl.
Row 13: Knit—25 sts.
Row 14: Change to D (E) and knit.
Row 15: Knit—23 sts.
Row 16: Purl.
Row 17: Knit—21 sts.
Row 18: Change to E (F) and knit.
Row 19: Knit—19 sts.
Row 20: Purl.
Row 21: Knit—17 sts.
Row 22: Change to A (A) and knit.
Row 23: Knit—15 sts.
Row 24: Purl.

Row 25: Knit—13 sts.
Row 26: Change to F (D) and knit.
Row 27: Knit—11 sts.
Row 28: Purl.
Row 29: Knit—9 sts.
Row 30: P3, p3tog-tbl, p3—7 sts.
Row 31: Knit—5 sts.
Row 32: P1, p3tog-tbl, p1—3 sts
Row 33: Sk2p—1 st.
Fasten off.

BOTTOM

Make 2 Square A's.
Put points C of squares together; with color B, pick up and knit 20 sts along side D–C of first square, then pick up and knit 19 sts along side C–B of 2nd square.
Knit 1 row.
Continue working Rows 1–33 of Square A.
Rep on other side of original squares.
You now have a large square made from 4 Square A's.

First Layer of Squares

With color G, pick up and knit 20 sts along side A–D of 1 square of bottom, then pick up and knit 19 sts along side B–A of adjoining square.
Knit 1 row.
Work Rows 1–33 of Square B.
Rep around, making 3 more Square B's.

2nd Layer of Squares

With color B, pick up and knit 20 sts along side A–D of 1 square of first layer, then pick up and knit 19 sts along side B–A of adjoining square.
Knit 1 row.
Work Rows 1–33 of Square A.
Rep around, making 3 more Square A's.

3rd Layer of Squares

Work as for first layer of squares.

FINISHING

Top border

With RS facing and color A, pick up and knit 18 sts along side B–A, then 18 sts along side A–D of first square in 3rd layer.
Rep along tops of rem squares on 3rd layer; place marker for beg of rnd and join—144 sts.
[Purl 1 rnd, knit 1 rnd] 4 times, purl 1 rnd. Bind off very loosely kwise.
Weave in all ends. Block to finished measurements.

To avoid the tangled mess of using several different color yarns, place one skein of each color inside a small drawstring bag. Pull out only the color you need. When you're done, snip off the yarn at the opening of the bag, leaving just an inch hanging out so you can see the color for later use.

STRAPS
Make 2

Cut 3 strands 30-inches long from each color except A.
Holding all strands tog, make an overhand knot near 1 end, leaving tails as fringe.
Divide strands into 3 mixed-color groups and braid.
Make an overhand knot in end, leaving tails as fringe.
Sew one knotted end and approx 1 inch of strap to one point of top border; sew other end to adjacent point.
Rep for other strap.

Lining (optional)

Fold fabric with RS together. Lay completed tote on top and trace around outside of bag. Sew ¼-inch seam, attach to bag around top opening. ■

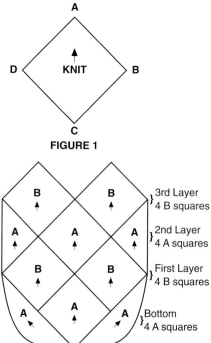

FIGURE 1

FIGURE 2

HARLEQUIN SOCKS

DESIGN BY KATHRYN BECKERDITE

WHAT'S IN THE BAG

Plymouth Yarn Happy Feet
  (sock weight; 90% superwash
  merino wool/10% nylon; 192
  yds/50g per skein): 3 skeins
  grape/garnet #5
Size 1 (2.25mm) double-point needles (set
  of 5) or size needed to obtain gauge
Size C/2 (2.75mm) crochet hook
Stitch marker

SKILL LEVEL

■■■□ INTERMEDIATE

SIZES

Woman's small (woman's large, man's small,
man's large) to fit woman's shoe sizes 6-7
(woman's 8-9, man's 8-9, man's 10–11)
Instructions are given for the smallest size,
with larger sizes in parentheses. When only
1 number is given, it applies to all sizes.

FINISHED MEASUREMENTS

Circumference: 8 (8¼, 8⅝, 8¾) inches
Foot length: 9 (9⅜, 9⅞, 10¼) inches

GAUGE

32 sts and 44 rnds =
4 inches/10cm in St st.
To save time, take time
to check gauge.

SPECIAL ABBREVIATIONS

Wrap and Turn (W&T):
Bring yarn to RS of
work between needles,
slip next st pwise to
RH needle, bring yarn
around this st to WS,
slip st back to LH needle,
turn work to begin
working back in the
other direction.

Work wrapped sts and wraps tog (WW): *On
RS:* Knit to wrapped st, slip the wrapped st
pwise from LH needle to RH needle. Use tip of
LH needle to pick up wrap(s) and place it/them
on RH needle. Slip wrap(s) and st back to LH
needle and knit
them tog.

On WS: Purl to wrapped st, slip the wrapped
st kwise from LH needle to RH needle. Use
tip of LH to pick up wrap(s) and place it/them
on RH needle. Slip wrap(s) and st back to LH
needle and purl them tog.

Make 1 (M1): Insert LH needle from front to
back under the running thread between the
last st worked and next st on LH needle. With
RH needle, knit into the back of this loop.

PATTERN STITCH

**Diamond Panel
(multiple of 15 sts over 26 rnds)**
Rnds 1 and 2: P7, k1, p7.
Rnds 3 and 4: P6, k1, p1, k1, p6.
Rnds 5 and 6: P5, (k1, p1) twice, k1, p5.
Rnds 7 and 8: P4, (k1, p1) 3 times, k1, p4.
Rnds 9 and 10: P3, (k1, p1, k1, p3) twice.
Rnds 11 and 12: P2, k1, p1, k1, p5, k1, p1, k1, p2.
Rnds 13 and 14: P1, k1, p1, k1, p7, k1, p1, k1, p1.
Rnds 15 and 16: Rep Rnds 11 and 12.
Rnds 17 and 18: Rep Rnds 9 and 10.
Rnds 19 and 20: Rep Rnds 7 and 8.
Rnds 21 and 22: Rep Rnds 5 and 6.
Rnds 23 and 24: Rep
Rnds 3 and 4.
Rnds 25 and 26: Rep
Rnds 1 and 2.
  Rep Rnds 1–26
for pat.

SPECIAL TECHNIQUES

**Provisional Cast-
On:** With crochet
hook and waste
yarn, make a chain
several sts longer
than desired cast
on. With knitting

29

needle and project yarn, pick up indicated number of sts in the "bumps" on back of chain. When indicated in pat, "unzip" the crochet chain to free live sts.

Sewn Bind-Off: Cut yarn, leaving a 1-yd tail. Using a tapestry needle, *thread the yarn pwise through the first 2 sts on the needle. Pull through, leaving the sts on the needle. Thread the yarn kwise through the first st on the needle, pull through. Drop the first st off the needle. Rep from * around.

PATTERN NOTES

This sock is worked on 4 double-point needles from the toe up, with short-row toe and heel shaping and ending with a Sewn Bind-Off.

A chart for the Diamond Panel is included for those preferring to work from charts.

SOCK

SHORT-ROW TOE

Using provisional method, cast on 32 (34, 36, 38) sts.

Row 1 (WS): Purl.
Row 2: Knit to last st, W&T.
Row 3: Purl to last st, W&T.
Row 4: Knit to st before last wrapped st, W&T.
Row 5: Purl to st before last wrapped st, W&T.

Rep Rows 4 and 5 until 12 (12, 14, 14) sts rem unwrapped.

Row 6: Knit to the first wrapped st, WW, W&T.
Row 7: Purl to the first wrapped st, WW, W&T.
Row 8: Knit to the first double-wrapped st, WW, W&T.
Row 9: Purl to the first double-wrapped st, WW, W&T.

Rep Rows 8 and 9 until one double-wrapped st rem at each end of work.
Row 10: Knit to double-wrapped st, knit double-wrapped st, do not turn; place marker for beg of rnd.

Unzip Provisional Cast-On and distribute newly live (instep) sts and sole sts evenly divided on 4 dpns—64 (68, 72, 76) total sts with 16 (17, 18, 19) sts on each needle.

FOOT

Rnd 1: Knit.
Rnd 2 (inc instep sts): K7 (8, 7, 8), [M1, k3] 6 (6, 7, 7) times, M1, knit to end—71 (75, 80, 84) sts.
Rnd 3: K5 (6, 5, 6), [p1, k1] 14 (14, 16, 16) times, p1, knit to end.

Rep Rnd 3 until piece measures approx 7¼ (7¾, 8, 8½) inches from beg.

SHORT-ROW HEEL

Turn work.

Leaving instep sts unworked, work heel as for toe over 32 (34, 36, 38) sole sts.

LEG

Rnd 1 (inc heel sts): Work instep sts in established pat; work heel sts as follows: k8, [M1, k3] 5 (5, 6, 6) times, k3, p7 (8, 7, 8)—76 (80, 86, 90) sts.
Rnd 2: *P8 (9, 8, 9), [k1, p1] 11 (11, 13, 13) times, k1, p7 (8, 7, 8); rep from * around.
Rnd 3: Work in established pat to last 7 (8, 7, 8) sts, place marker for new beg of rnd. Redistribute sts as desired.
Rnd 4: *P0 (1, 0, 1), work Diamond Panel over next 15 sts, p0 (1, 0, 1), [k1, p1] 11 (11, 13, 13) times, k1; rep from * around.

Continue in established pat and work Diamond Panel 3 times total.

Last 2 rnds: *P15 (17, 15, 17), [k1, p1] 11 (11, 13, 13) times; rep from * once.

Bind off using Sewn Bind-Off.

FINISHING

Weave in ends. Block. ∎

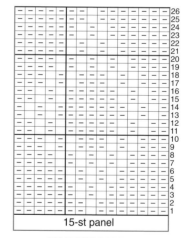

15-st panel

DIAMOND PANEL

STITCH KEY
☐ Knit
⊟ Purl

Socks couldn't be easier to take on the go. If your pattern calls for double-point needles, try a 12 inch circular needle instead. You can neatly store away your project, without those needles poking out at you!

TRAVELING LACE BEADED SHAWL

DESIGN BY CHRISTINE L. WALTER

WHAT'S IN THE BAG

Berroco Ultra Alpaca (worsted
  weight; 50% alpaca/50% wool;
  215 yds/100g per hank): 3 hank
  lavender mix #6283

4 MEDIUM

38 Mill Hill Pebble Beads size 3/0 in
  midnight rainbow #05086
Size 10½ (6.5mm) circular needle or size
  needed to obtain gauge
One blunt tapestry needle small enough to
  fit through beads

SKILL LEVEL

■■■□ INTERMEDIATE

FINISHED SIZE

Approx 20 x 62 inches

GAUGE

12 sts and 17 rows = 4 inches/10cm in Traveling
Lace pat (after blocking).
To save time, take time to check gauge.

SPECIAL ABBREVIATION

Bring Up Bead (BUB): Slide a bead up against
the st just worked.

PATTERN STITCH

Traveling Lace Pat (multiple of 10 sts + 1)
Row 1 (RS): K1, *yo, k8, k2tog; rep from *
across.
Row 2 and all WS rows: Purl.
Row 3: K1, *k1, yo, k7, k2tog; rep from * across.
Row 5: K1, *k2, yo, k6, k2tog; rep from * across.
Row 7: K1, *k3, yo, k5, k2tog; rep from * across.
Row 9: K1, *k4, yo, k4, k2tog; rep from * across.
Row 11: K1, *k5, yo, k3, k2tog; rep from * across.
Row 13: K1, *k6, yo, k2, k2tog; rep from * across.
Row 15: K1, *k7, yo, k1, k2tog; rep from * across.
Row 17: K1, *k8, yo, k2tog; rep from * across.
Row 19: *Ssk, k8, yo; rep from * to last st, k1.
Row 21: *Ssk, k7, yo, k1; rep from * to last st, k1.
Row 23: *Ssk, k6, yo, k2; rep from * to last st, k1.
Row 25: *Ssk, k5, yo, k3; rep from * to last st, k1.

Row 27: *Ssk, k4, yo, k4; rep from * to last st, k1.
Row 29: *Ssk, k3, yo, k5; rep from * to last st, k1.
Row 31: *Ssk, k2, yo, k6; rep from * to last st, k1.
Row 33: *Ssk, k1, yo, k7; rep from * to last st, k1.
Row 35: *Ssk, yo, k8; rep from * to last st, k1.
Row 36: Purl.
  Rep Rows 1–36 for pat.

PATTERN NOTES

Purchase extra beads because some beads may have bad center holes.

A chart is provided for those preferring to work from charts.

SHAWL

Measure off approx 50 inches of yarn, make a slip knot and place on needle.

String 19 beads on the 50-inch tail.

Beaded cast-on row: Using Long-Tail Cast-On method, BUB, [cast on 3 sts, BUB] 18 times, cast on 1 st—56 sts.

Knit 7 rows, increasing 1 st on last row—57 sts.

Row 1 (RS): K3, work Row 1 of Traveling Lace pat, k3.

Row 2: K3, purl to last 3 sts, k3.

Continue working first and last 3 sts in garter st and working Traveling Lace pat between

Tip In social settings, avoid patterns that require excessive counting of rows or stitches. Instead, find easy projects with no shaping and simple stitch patterns.

markers as established.

Work 8 complete reps of Traveling Lace pat.

Knit 7 rows, decreasing 1 st on first row—56 sts.

Cut yarn, leaving a 50-inch tail.

With RS facing, working from left to right, using small tapestry needle and keeping the working yarn above, thread a bead onto the yarn and BUB; *go into the 2nd st from the front, then into the first st from the back; pull the yarn through both sts; slip the first st off the needle; rep from * twice more omitting the bead and keeping the tension fairly loose. Continue binding off in this manner, introducing a bead every 3rd maneuver until 19 beads have been placed and all sts have been bound off.

FINISHING

Weave in ends. Block to finished measurements. ■

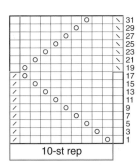

								o		＼	31
							o			＼	29
						o				＼	27
					o					＼	25
				o						＼	23
			o							＼	21
		o								＼	19
／	o										17
／		o									15
／			o								13
／				o							11
／					o						9
／						o					7
／							o				5
／								o			3
／									o		1

10-st rep

STITCH KEY
☐ K on RS
◉ Yo
⟋ K2tog
⟍ Ssk
Note: This 32-row chart shows RS rows only. Purl all WS rows.

TRAVELING LACE

GOSSAMER CAPELET

DESIGN BY LAURA BRYANT FOR PRISM YARN

WHAT'S IN THE BAG

Prism Gossamer (lace weight; 80% kid mohair/20% nylon; 935 yds/100g per skein): 1 skein gelato

Size 8 (5mm) needles or size needed to obtain gauge
Stitch markers
1 large button
1 small button

SKILL LEVEL

 INTERMEDIATE

SIZE
One size fits most

FINISHED MEASUREMENTS
Circumference: As desired by knitter
Length: Approx 22 inches

GAUGE
18 sts and 28 rows = 4 inches/10cm in garter st with 2 strands held together.

To save time, take time to check gauge.

PATTERN NOTES
This capelet is worked sideways in garter stitch, with very loose stitches worked with multiple wraps at one side (the bottom as worn) and regular knit stitches at the other side (the neck as worn); all extra wraps from previous rows are dropped as new stitches are formed.

It is critical that cast on and bind off be very loose.

Two strands of yarn are held together throughout.

CAPELET
Cast on 11 sts, place marker; cast on 22 sts, place marker; cast on 33 sts, place marker—66 sts.

Set-up row (RS): [K1, wrapping yarn around needle 3 times; drop next 2 sts from needle] 11 times; [k1, wrapping yarn around needle twice; drop next st from needle] 11 times; k11—33 sts.

Row 1: K11; k11, wrapping yarn around needle twice and dropping extra yo's from previous row; k11, wrapping yarn around needle 3 times and dropping yo's from previous row–33 sts.

Row 2: K11, wrapping yarn around needle 3 times and dropping yo's; k11, wrapping yarn around needle twice and dropping extra yo's; k11.

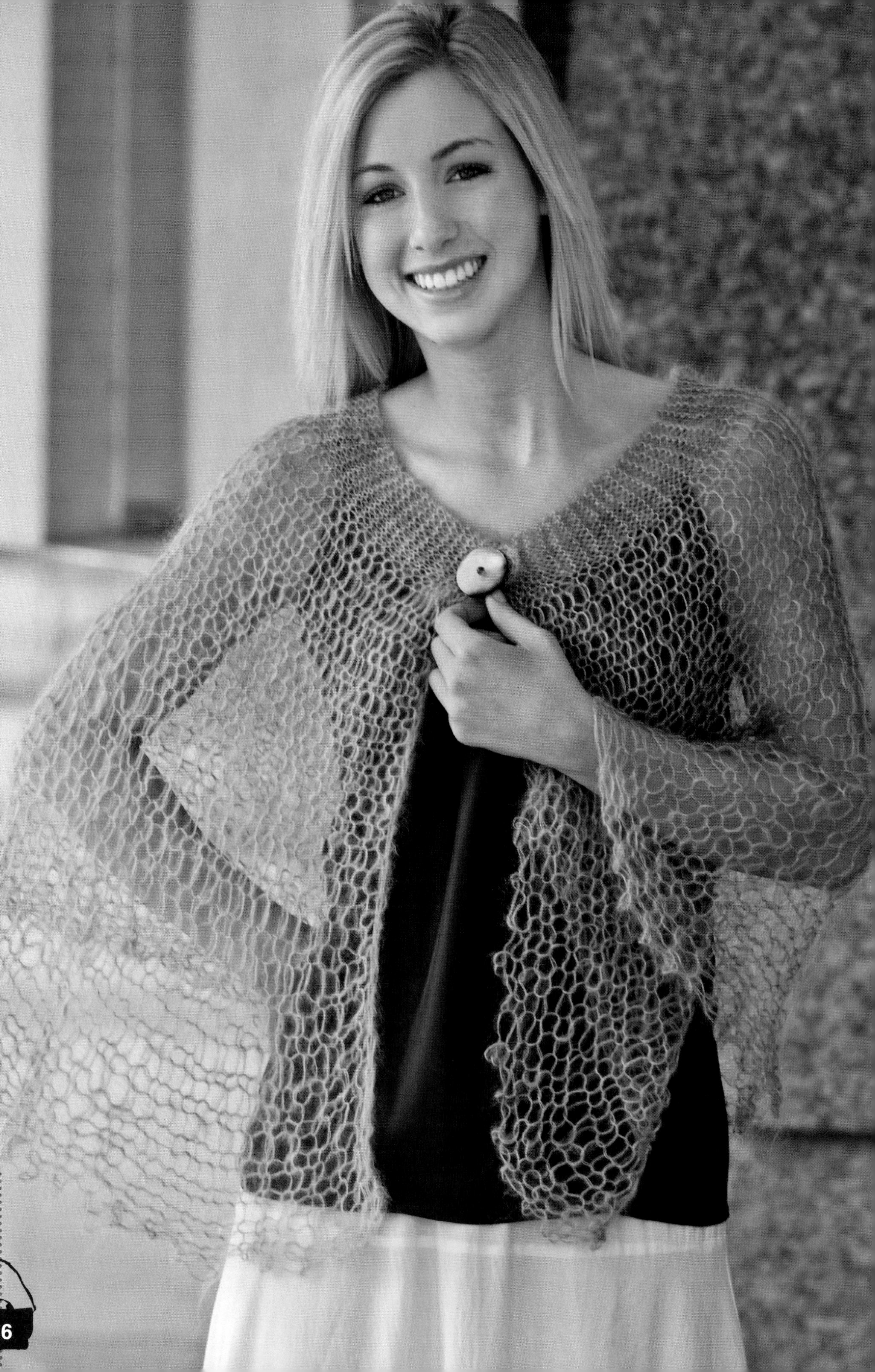

"While visiting India, I ventured out on a harrowing bus tour from Delhi to Jaipur. We wound our way up the two-lane road barely missing goats, carts and children. However, I was oblivious—engaged with a P.D. James mystery on tape and engrossed in an entrelac coat. Taking notice of my interest in knitting, our tour guide made certain that we saw local textile businesses in each city where we stayed. We visited a rug manufacturer, an embroidery studio, a crafts museum, and we had a private tour of a hand weaving studio. It's amazing the worlds that knitting can open."

Rep Rows 1 and 2, dropping extra yo's from needle on each row until short edge (neckline) measures approx 26 inches when laid flat and pulled straight.

Try capelet on and work more rows if desired for additional width, ending with Row 2.

Next row (RS): Make buttonhole in center of first 11 sts (size will depend on size of your large button), work to end of row.

Work 4 rows in established pat.

Removing all markers, bind off as follows: Dropping yo's from previous row as you knit, [k1; yo, pass st over yo; yo, pass st over yo] 11 times; [k1, pass st over previous st, yo, pass st over yo] 11 times; bind off rem sts.

FINISHING

Block as necessary.

Sew larger button to left front, sewing through capelet and then through 2nd, smaller button on the inside (to provide support). ■

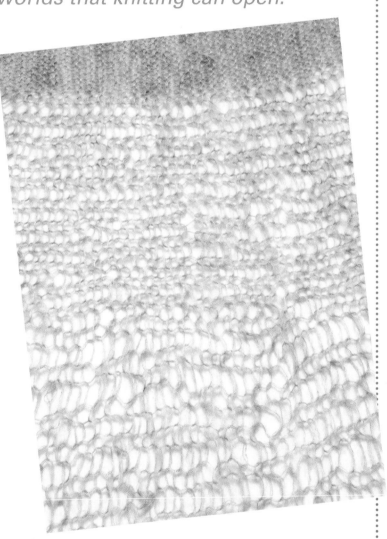

WANDERING WEARABLES

You'll enjoy our refreshing selection of garments with clever and easy stitch designs, making it a breeze to bring your project along on that morning hike. Take a break, enjoy the scenery and knit a few rows!

DUAL TEXTURE TUNIC

DESIGN BY MELISSA LEAPMAN

WHAT'S IN THE BAG

Ornaghi Filati United (worsted weight; 55% bamboo/45% cotton; 92 yds/50g per ball): 10 (11, 12, 12, 13) balls earth #518

Size 6 (4mm) needles or size needed to obtain gauge

SKILL LEVEL
■■□□ EASY

SIZES
Woman's small (medium, large, extra-large, 2X-large) Instructions are given for smallest size, with larger sizes in parentheses. When only 1 number is given, it applies to all sizes.

FINISHED MEASUREMENTS
Chest: 32 (36, 40, 43, 47) inches
Length: 30 (31, 32, 33, 34) inches

GAUGE
20 sts and 25 rows = 4 inches/10cm in St st.
22 sts and 30 rows = 4 inches/10cm in Double Seed st.
To save time, take time to check gauge.

PATTERN STITCH
Double Seed St
(even number of sts)
Row 1 (RS): *K1, p1; rep from * across.
Row 2: Rep Row 1.
Rows 3 and 4: *P1, k1; rep from * across.
   Rep Rows 1–4 for pat.

PATTERN NOTE
Work all shaping decreases 1 stitch

from the edge, working the edge stitch in Stockinette stitch. On right side rows, work slip, slip, knit decrease at beginning of rows and knit 2 together decrease at end of rows; on wrong side rows, work purl 2 together decrease at beginning of rows and slip, slip, purl decrease at end of rows.

BACK
Cast on 95 (105, 115, 125, 135) sts.
   Work even in St st until piece measures approx 18½ (19¼, 20, 20¾, 21½) inches allowing lower edge to curl, ending with a RS row.

Empire Waist
Next Row (WS): Purl, dec 7 (5, 5, 7, 5) sts evenly across row—88 (100, 110, 118, 130) sts.
   Work even in Double Seed st until piece measures 22 (22½, 23, 23½, 24) inches, ending with a WS row.

Shape armholes
Bind off 5 (6, 7, 7, 8) sts at beg of next 2 rows, then bind off 2 (2, 3, 3, 4) sts at beg of following 2 rows—74 (84, 90, 98, 106) sts.
   Dec 1 st each side [every row] 0 (0, 2, 6, 10) times, [every other row] 1 (8, 8, 7, 6) time(s), then [every 4th row] 3 (0, 0, 0, 0) times—66 (68, 70, 72, 74) sts.
   Work even in established pat until armholes measure approx 6½ (7, 7½, 8, 8½) inches, ending with a WS row.

Shape neck
Next Row (RS): Work across first 15 (16, 17, 18, 19) sts; join 2nd ball of yarn and bind off center 36 sts, work to end of row.
   Working both sides at once with

separate balls of yarn, dec 1 st at each neck edge once—14 (15, 16, 17, 18) sts each side.

Work even until armholes measure approx 7 (7½, 8, 8½, 9) inches, ending with a WS row.

Shape shoulders
Bind off 4 (4, 4, 4, 5) sts at beg (armhole edge) of next 6 rows, then bind off 2 (3, 4, 5, 3) sts at beg of following 2 rows.

FRONT
Work as for back until armholes measure approx 1½ (2, 2½, 3, 3½) inches, ending with a WS row.

Shape neck
Continue armhole shaping same as for back and at the same time, shape neck as follows:

Next row (RS): Join 2nd ball of yarn and bind off center 16 sts, then work to end of row.

Working both sides at once with separate balls of yarn, bind off at each neck edge as follows: 4 sts once, 3 sts once, 2 sts once.

Dec 1 st at each neck edge [every row] twice—14 (15, 16, 17, 18) sts each side.

Work even until piece measures same as back to shoulders.

Shape shoulders
Work same as for back.

FINISHING
Block pieces to finished measurements. Sew right shoulder seam.

Neckband
With RS facing, pick up and knit 163 sts along neckline.
    Work 7 rows in St st.
    Bind off loosely, allowing neckband to roll to RS.
    Sew left shoulder seam, including side of neckband.

Armbands
With RS facing, pick up and knit 90 (98, 106, 114, 122) sts along armhole.
    Work as for neckband.

Sew side seams, including side of armbands. Weave in all ends. ■

FRONT

3 (3¼, 3½, 3¾, 4)"
7"
5"
1"
7 (7½, 8, 8½, 9)"
22 (22½, 23, 23½, 24)"
29 (30, 31, 32, 33)"
16 (18, 20, 21½, 23½)"
19 (21, 23, 25, 27)"

BACK

3 (3¼, 3½, 3¾, 4)"
7"
1½"
1"
7 (7½, 8, 8½, 9)"
22 (22½, 23, 23½, 24)"
29 (30, 31, 32, 33)"
16 (18, 20, 21½, 23½)"
19 (21, 23, 25, 27)"

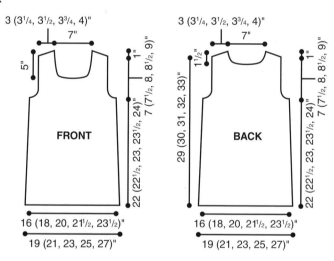

Tip Fill a compact-sized make-up bag with various-size circular needles, notions, travel scissors, tapestry needles and stitch holders. This bag can easily be moved from one knitting bag to another so you're never without your supplies.

EUROPEAN TOUR SET

DESIGNS BY KATE ATHERLEY

WHAT'S IN THE BAG

Knit One Crochet Too Soxx
    Appeal (fingering weight; 96%
    superwash merino wool/3%
    nylon/1% elastic; 208 yds/50g
    per ball): 4 (4, 5, 6, 7) balls lavender
    cream #9122

 1 SUPER FINE

Size 4 (3.5mm) 16- and 24-inch circular
    needles or size needed to obtain gauge
Stitch markers

SKILL LEVEL

■■■□ INTERMEDIATE

VEST

VEST SIZES

Woman's extra-small (small, medium, large,
extra-large) Instructions are given for smallest
size, with larger sizes in parentheses. When
only 1 number is given, it applies to all sizes.

FINISHED MEASUREMENTS

Chest: 30 (34, 38, 42, 46) inches
Length to shoulder: 19¼ (20¾, 21¾, 22¾, 24)
inches

GAUGE

28 sts and 44
rnds = 4 inches/
10cm in St st.
To save time,
take time to check
gauge.

SPECIAL ABBREVIATIONS

**Slip, slip, slip, knit
(sssk):** Slip next 3
sts 1 at a time kwise,
then knit the 3 slipped
sts tog—a left-leaning
double dec.

Wrap and Turn (W&T): Bring yarn to RS of
work between needles, slip next st pwise to RH
needle, bring yarn around this st to WS, slip st
back to LH needle, turn work to begin working
back in the other direction.

SPECIAL TECHNIQUE

3-Needle Bind-Off: With RS tog and needles
parallel, using a 3rd needle, knit tog a st from
the front needle with 1 from the back. *Knit tog
a st from the front and back needles, and slip
the first st over the 2nd to bind off. Rep from *
across, then fasten off last st.

PATTERN NOTE

Neck and armhole shaping occurs at different
rates for different sizes; where the letters "xx"
appear instead of stitch count numbers, it
means that these sizes are not being worked
on these rows.

BODY

Using the longer circular needle, cast on
212 (240, 268, 296, 324) sts; place marker to
indicate beg of rnd and join, taking care not to
twist sts.
    Work K3, P1 Rib for 1½ (1½, 1¾, 2, 2¼) inches.
    Change to St st and work even until piece
measures 12 (13, 13½, 14, 14½) inches.

Divide for front & back
Next rnd: Bind off 1 st,
k104 (118, 132, 146, 160)
including st rem from
bind off, bind off 2 sts,
k104 (118, 132, 146, 160)
including st rem from
bind off, bind off 1 st.

BACK

Row 1 (RS): With
shorter circular needle,
pick up and knit 1 st
in first bound-off st,
p1, k1, p1, sssk, knit
to last 6 sts, k3tog,

"Once, on flight across the Atlantic, I was knitting a cabled sweater made on circular needles. When taking breaks, I tend to tuck my needles in the neckline of my top. When it came time to land, I packed away my project, deplaned, proceeded through customs, picked up my luggage, and took a taxi to the hotel. Not until getting ready to shower and change did I realize that the big green cable needle was still tucked neatly into my V-neck t-shirt!"

p1, k1, p1; pick up and knit 1 st in first of the 2 bound-off sts—102 (116, 130, 144, 158) back sts. Leave rem 104 (118, 132, 146, 160) sts on longer circular needle to hold for front.
Row 2 and all WS rows: Sl 1, k1, p1, k1, purl to last 4 sts, k1, p1, k1, p1.

Shape Armholes
For sizes S, M, L, XL only
Dec row (RS): Sl 1, p1, k1, p1, sssk, knit to last 7 sts, k3tog, p1, k1, p1, k1—xx (112, 126, 140, 154) sts.
Rep Dec row [every other row] 0 (0 1, 1, 1) time more—xx (112, 122, 136, 150) sts.
For all sizes
Dec row (RS): Sl 1, p1, k1, p1, ssk, knit to last 6 sts, k2tog, p1, k1, p1, k1—100 (110, 120, 134, 148) sts
Rep Dec row [every other row] 8 (8, 9, 11, 13) more times—84 (94, 102, 112, 122) sts.
Maintaining first and last 4 sts in established rib, work even until armhole measures 6¾ (7¼, 7¾, 8¼, 9) inches, ending with a WS row.

Back Neck
Row 1 (RS): Work 20 (25, 28, 32, 34) sts in established pat, place marker, [p1, k1] 11 (11, 11, 12, 13) times, M1, [k1, p1] 11 (11, 12, 12, 14) times, place marker, work in established pat to end of row—85 (95, 103, 113, 123) sts.
Row 2: Slipping markers, work in pat to marker, work in established rib to next marker, work in pat to end of row.
Work even for 4 rows.

Shape Shoulders
Row 1 (RS): Work in pat to last 7 (9, 10, 11, 12) sts, W&T.
Row 2: Work in pat to last 7 (9, 10, 11, 12) sts, W&T.
Row 3: Work in pat to last 14 (17, 19, 22, 23) sts, W&T.

Row 4: Work in pat to last 14 (17, 19, 22, 23) sts, W&T.
Row 5: Work in pat to last 20 (25, 28, 32, 34) W&T.
Row 6: Bind off 45 (45, 47, 49, 55) rib sts in pat, turn.
Cut yarn.
Slip back shoulder sts to longer needle and front sts to shorter needle.

DIVIDE FOR LEFT & RIGHT FRONTS
With RS facing, rejoin yarn to front sts.
Next rnd: Pick up and knit 1 st in bound-off st at beg of row, p1, k1, p1, sssk, k45 (52, 59, 66, 72), bind off 2 sts, k45 (52, 59, 66, 73) including st rem from bind off, k3tog, p1, k1, p1, pick up and knit 1 st in bound-off st at end of row; slip left front sts to the longer circular needle to hold for later—50 (57, 64, 71, 78) right front sts.

RIGHT FRONT
Shape Armholes and V-Neck
Row 1 (WS): Sl 1, k1, p1, k1, purl to last 3 sts, k1, p1, k1.
Row 2 (XS only): Pick up 1 st in 2nd bound-off st, p1, k1, p1, knit to last 6 sts, k2tog, p1, k1, p1, k1—50 sts.
Row 2 (S, M, L, XL only): Pick up 1 st in 2nd bound-off st, p1, k1, p1, knit to last 7 sts, k3tog, p1, k1, p1, k1—xx (56, 63, 70, 77) sts.
Row 3 and all WS rows: Sl 1, k1, p1, k1, purl to last 4 sts, k1, p1, k1, p1.
Row 4 (XS and S only): Sl 1, p1, k1, p1, ssk, knit to last 6 sts, k2tog, p1, k1, p1, k1—48 (54, xx, xx, xx) sts.
Row 4 (M, L, XL only): Sl 1, p1, k1, p1, ssk, knit to last 7 sts, k3tog, p1, k1, p1, k1—xx (xx, 60, 67, 74) sts.
Row 5: Sl 1, p1, k1, p1, knit to last 6 sts, k2tog, p1, k1, p1, k1—47 (53, 59, 66, 73) sts.
Continue in pat as established, dec 1 inside

armhole ribbing [every RS row] 6 (7, 9, 11, 13) times and dec 1 inside neck ribbing [every other RS row] 17 (17, 18, 19, 22) times—24 (29, 32, 36, 38) sts.

Work even, maintaining rib on first and last 4 sts of the rows, until front measures same as back to shoulder shaping, ending with a WS row.

Shape Shoulders
Row 1 (RS): Work in pat to last 7 (9, 10, 11, 12) sts, W&T.
Rows 2, 4, 6: Work even.
Row 3: Work in pat to last 14 (17, 19, 22, 23) sts, W&T.
Row 5: Work in pat to last 20 (25, 28, 32, 34) sts, W&T.

Slip right front sts to the longer circular needle.

Left Front
Slip 50 (57, 64, 71, 78) left front sts from the longer needle to shorter needle.

With WS facing, rejoin yarn.

Shape Armholes and V-Neck
Row 1 (WS): Sl 1, k1, p1, k1, purl to last 3 sts, k1, p1, k1.
Row 2 (XS only): K1, p1, k1, p1, ssk, knit to last 3 sts, p1, k1, p1, pick up 1 st in bound-off st —50 sts.
Row 2 (S, M, L, XL only): K1, p1, k1, p1, sssk, knit to last 4 sts, p1, k1, p1, k1, pick up 1 st in bound-off st—xx (56, 63, 70, 77) sts.
Row 3 and all WS rows: Sl 1, k1, p1, k1, purl to last 4 sts, k1, p1, k1, p1.
Row 4 (XS and S only): Sl 1, p1, k1, p1, ssk, knit to last 6 sts, k2tog, p1, k1, p1, k1—48 (54, xx, xx, xx) sts.
Row 4 (M, L, XL only): Sl 1, p1, k1, p1, sssk, knit

to last 7 sts, k2tog, p1, k1, p1, k1—xx (xx, 58, 67, 74) sts.
Row 5: Sl 1, p1, k1, p1, ssk, knit to last 4 sts, p1, k1, p1, k1—47 (53, 59, 66, 73) sts.

Continue in pat as established, dec 1 inside armhole ribbing [every RS row] 6 (7, 9, 11, 13) times and dec 1 inside neck ribbing [every other RS row] 17 (17, 18, 19, 22) times—24 (29, 32, 36, 38) sts.

Work even, maintaining rib on first and last 4 sts of the rows, until front measures same as back to shoulder shaping, ending with a WS row.

Shape Shoulders
Row 1 (WS): Work in pat to last 7 (9, 10, 11, 12) sts, W&T.
Rows 2, 4, 6 (RS): Work even.
Row 3 (WS): Work in pat to last 14 (17, 19, 22, 23) sts, W&T.
Row 5 (WS): Work in pat to last 20 (25, 28, 32, 34) sts, W&T.

FINISHING
Slip sts for right shoulder back to shorter needle.

Join front and back shoulder sts using 3-Needle Bind-Off.

Weave in ends.

Block to finished measurements.

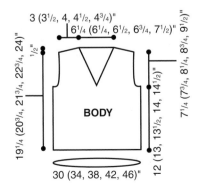

3 (3½, 4, 4½, 4¾)"

6¼ (6¼, 6½, 6¾, 7½)"

½"

19¼ (20¾, 21¾, 22¾, 24)"

7¼ (7¾, 8¼, 8¾, 9½)"

BODY

12 (13, 13½, 14, 14½)"

30 (34, 38, 42, 46)"

SOCKS

WHAT'S IN THE BAG

Knit One Crochet Too Soxx
Appeal (fingering weight; 96%
superwash merino wool/3%
nylon/1% elastic; 208 yds/50g
per ball): 1 (2, 2) balls lavender cream
#9122
Size 1 (2.5mm) double-point needles (set
of 4 or 5) or size needed to obtain gauge
Stitch marker

1 SUPER FINE

SOCKS SIZES

Woman's small (medium, large) to fit shoe
sizes 5-7 (7-9, 10+) Instructions are given for
smallest size, with larger sizes in parentheses.
When only 1 number is given, it applies to all
sizes.

FINISHED MEASUREMENTS

Circumference: 7¼ (7¾, 8¼) inches
Foot length: 8 (8½, 9) inches

GAUGE

32 sts and 48 rnds = 4 inches/10cm in St st.
To save time, take time to check gauge.

SPECIAL ABBREVIATION
N1, N2, N3: Needle 1, Needle 2, Needle 3

PATTERN NOTE
Due to the elastic in the yarn, the fabric has a
lot of vertical stretch. The finished sock foot
will seem shorter than you would normally
work in a non-stretch yarn.

INSTRUCTIONS
Cast on 58 (62, 66) sts; distribute evenly on
3 dpn; place marker for beg of rnd and join,
being careful not to twist sts.
 Work in K1, P1 Rib for 1 inch.

Heel flap
Row 1 (RS): K29 (31, 33) heel sts and turn,
leaving rem 29 (31, 33) instep sts on hold on
single dpn.
 Work heel sts in St st for 21 (23, 23) rows,
ending with a WS row.

Turn heel
Row 1 (RS): K19 (21, 22), ssk, turn.
Row 2: Sl 1, p9 (11, 11), p2tog, turn.
Row 3: Sl 1, k9 (11, 11), ssk, turn.
 Rep Rows 2 and 3 until all sts have been
worked, ending with a WS row—11 (13, 13) sts
rem.

Gusset
Rnd 1: With N1, k11 (13, 13) heel sts, then pick
up and knit 15 (16, 16) along heel flap; with N2,
knit across 29 (31, 33) instep sts; with N3, pick
up and knit 15 (16, 16) sts along heel flap, then
k6 (7, 7) sts heel sts, place marker for beg of
rnd—70 (76, 78) sts with 20 (22, 22) sts on N1,
29 (31, 33) sts on N2 and 21 (23, 23) sts on N3.
Rnd 2: Knit around, working all picked up
sts tbl.
Rnd 3 (dec): N1: Knit to last 3 sts, k2tog, k1; N2:
knit; N3: k1, ssk, knit to end—68 (74, 76) sts.
Rnd 4: Knit.
 Rep [Rnds 3 and 4] 5 (6, 5) times—58 (62, 66)
sts with 14 (15, 16) sts on N1, 29 (31, 33) sts on
N2 and 15 (16, 17) sts on N3.

Foot
Work even in St st until foot measures 6 (6½, 7)
inches from back of heel.

Toe
Dec rnd: N1: Knit to last 3 sts, k2tog, k1; N2: k1,
ssk, knit to last 3 sts, k2tog, k1; N3: k1, ssk, knit

to end—54 (58, 62) sts.

Work Dec rnd [every 3rd rnd] 3 times—42 (46, 50) sts.

Work Dec rnd [every other rnd] 3 times—30 (34, 38) sts.

Work Dec rnd [every rnd] 5 (6, 7) times—10 sts.

Cut yarn and using the crochet hook or yarn needle, pull through remaining sts to close. Weave in ends.

FINISHING

Soak socks in lukewarm water for a few minutes, roll in a towel to wring out and then put them on. Take them off again, and leave them to air dry. This blocks the socks to ensure a good fit.

SCARF

WHAT'S IN THE BAG

Knit One Crochet Too Soxx Appeal (fingering weight; 96% superwash merino wool/3% nylon/1% elastic; 208 yds/50g per ball): 4 balls lavender cream #9122
Size 4 (3.5mm) 24-inch circular needle or size needed to obtain gauge

1 SUPER FINE

SCARF FINISHED SIZE
Approx 16 x 48 inches

GAUGE
26 sts and 36 rows = 4 inches/10cm in lace rib pattern using larger needles.
To save time, take time to check gauge.

PATTERN STITCH
Lace Rib (multiple of 6 sts + 2)
Row 1: K1, *yo, SK2P, yo, k1, p1, k1; rep from * to last st, k1.
Rep Row 1 for pat.

PATTERN NOTE
To make scarf wider, cast on more stitches in multiples of 6.

INSTRUCTIONS
Cast on 104 sts.
Work even in Lace Rib pat for approx 48 inches or until you've just about run out of yarn.

To bind off, lift the sts 1 by 1 over each other, without working them.

Weave in ends and block. ■

CASUAL COTTON T-SHIRT

DESIGN BY AVA LYNNE GREEN

WHAT'S IN THE BAG

Rowan Wool Cotton (DK weight; 50% merino wool/50% cotton; 123 yds/50g per ball): 6 (7, 8, 9, 10) balls pumpkins #962

Size 5 (3.75mm) needles or size needed to obtain gauge

SKILL LEVEL

 INTERMEDIATE

SIZES

Woman's extra-small (small, medium, large, extra-large) Instructions are given for smallest size, with larger sizes in parentheses. When only 1 number is given, it applies to all sizes.

FINISHED MEASUREMENTS

Chest: 32 (36, 40, 44, 48) inches
Length to shoulder: 21 (22, 23, 24, 24) inches

GAUGE

20 sts and 27 rows = 4 inches/10cm in St st.
To save time, take time to check gauge.

SPECIAL ABBREVIATION

Make 1 (M1): Insert LH needle from front to back under the running thread between the last st worked and next st on RH needle; knit into the back of resulting loop.

PATTERN STITCH

Seed Stitch
Row 1 (RS): *K1, p1; rep from * to end.
Row 2: Knit the purl sts and purl the knit sts as they present themselves.
    Rep Row 2 for pat.

FRONT

Cast on 60 (70, 80, 90, 100) sts.
Rows 1 (RS)–3: Work in Seed st.
Row 4 (inc row): Work 3 sts in Seed st, M1, purl to the last 3 sts, M1, work 3 sts in Seed st—62 (72, 82, 92, 102) sts.
Row 5: Work 3 sts in Seed st, knit to the last 3 sts, work 3 sts in Seed st.
    Rep [Rows 4 and 5] 9 times—80 (90, 100, 110, 120) sts.
    Discontinue Seed st border and work even in St st until piece measures 13 (14, 14, 15, 15) inches, ending with a WS row.

Shape armhole
Row 1 (RS): K1, M1, knit to last st, M1, k1—82 (92, 102, 112, 122) sts.
Row 2: Purl.
Rows 3–6: Rep [Rows 1 and 2] twice—86 (96, 106, 116, 126) sts.
    Work even in St st until armholes measure 5 (5, 6, 6, 6) inches, ending with a WS row.

Shape front neck
Row 1 (RS): K34 (37, 42, 46, 50), join a 2nd ball

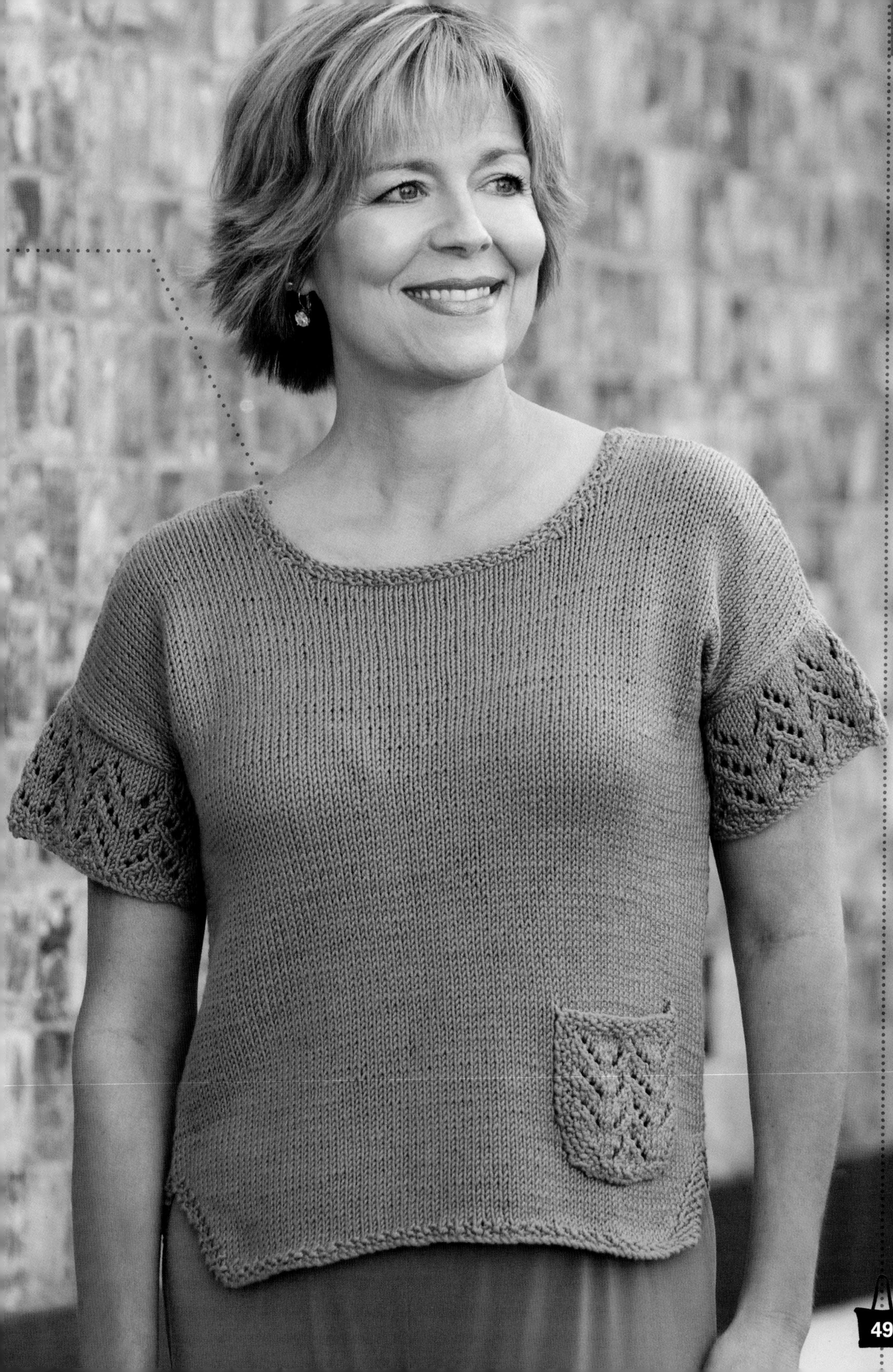

"Getting stranded at an airport for 5 hours due to bad weather was an ironic stroke of good luck! I found a cozy corner, pulled out my knitting and made great progress on a 3-color, top-down raglan sweater design. To this day, I think of it fondly as my airport sweater."

of yarn and bind off center 18 (22, 22, 24, 26) sts, knit to end.

Row 2: Working both sides at once with separate balls of yarn, purl across.

Row 3 (dec row): Knit to 3 sts before neck, k2tog, k1; k1, ssk, knit to end—33 (36, 41, 45, 49) sts each side.

Rep [Rows 2 and 3] 3 (3, 5, 6, 7) times—30 (33, 36, 39, 42) sts each side.

Work even until armholes measure 8 (8, 9, 9, 9) inches.

Bind off 10 (11, 12, 13, 14) sts at beg (armhole edge) of next 6 rows.

BACK

Cast on 60 (70, 80, 90, 100) sts.

Work as for front until armholes measure 6 (6, 7, 7, 7) inches, ending with a WS row.

Shape back neck

Row 1 (RS): K32 (35, 40, 44, 47), join a 2nd ball of yarn and bind off center 22 (26, 26, 28, 32) sts, knit to end.

Row 2: Working both sides at once with separate balls of yarn, purl across.

Row 3 (dec row): Knit to 3 sts before neck, k2tog, k1; k1, ssk, knit to end—31 (34, 39, 43, 46) sts each side.

Rep [Rows 2 and 3] 1 (1, 3, 4, 4) times—30 (33, 36, 39, 42) sts each shoulder.

Work even until piece measures same as front to shoulders.

Bind off 10 (11, 12, 13, 14) sts at beg (armhole edge) of next 6 rows.

SLEEVE

Cast on 64 (64, 72, 72, 72) sts.
Rows 1 (RS)–3: Work in Seed St.
Rows 4, 6, 8 and 10: Work 3 sts in Seed st, purl to last 3 sts, work 3 sts in Seed st.
Row 5: Work 3 sts in Seed st, M1, *k2, yo, ssk, k2, k2tog, yo; rep from * to last 5 sts, k2, M1, work 3 sts in Seed st—66 (66, 74, 74, 74) sts.
Row 7: Work 3 sts in Seed st, M1, k4, *yo, ssk, k2tog, yo, k4; rep from * to last 3 sts, M1, work 3 sts in Seed st—68 (68, 76, 76, 76) sts.
Row 9: Work 3 sts in Seed st, M1, k6, *yo, ssk, k6; rep from * to last 3 sts, M1, work 3 sts in Seed st—70 (70, 78, 78, 78) sts.
Row 11: K4, k2tog, yo, *k2, yo, ssk, k2, k2tog, yo; rep from * to last 8 sts, k2, yo, ssk, k4.
Row 12 and all rem WS rows: Purl.
Row 13: K3, k2tog, yo, *k4, yo, ssk, k2tog, yo; rep from * to last 9 sts, k4, yo, ssk, k3.
Row 15: K2, k2tog, yo, k6, *yo, ssk, k6; rep from * to last 4 sts, yo, ssk, k2.
Rows 17–22: Rep Rows 11-16.
Row 23: Knit.
Row 24: Purl.
Bind off.

POCKET

Cast on 16 sts.
Rows 1 (RS)–3: Work in Seed st.
Row 4 and all WS rows: Work 3 sts in Seed st, purl to last 3 sts, work 3 sts in Seed st.

Row 5: Work 3 sts in Seed st, M1, k2, yo, ssk, k2, k2tog, yo, k2, M1, work 3 sts in Seed st—18 sts.
Row 7: Work 3 sts in Seed st, M1, k4, yo, ssk, k2tog, M1, k4, work 3 sts in Seed st—20 sts.
Row 9: Work 3 sts in Seed st, M1, k6, yo, ssk, k6, M1, work 3 sts in Seed st—22 sts.
Row 11: Work 3 sts in Seed st, k1, k2tog, yo, k2, yo, ssk, k2, k2tog, yo, k2, yo, ssk, k1, work 3 sts in Seed st.
Row 13: Work 3 sts in Seed st, k2tog, yo, k4, yo, ssk, k2tog, yo, k4, yo, ssk, work 3 sts in Seed st.
Row 15: Work 2 sts in Seed st, k2tog, yo, k6, yo, ssk, k6, yo, ssk, work 2 sts in Seed st.
Rows 17–28: Rep [Rows 11-16] twice.
Rows 29–31: Work in Seed st.

FINISHING

Weave in all ends. Block all pieces to finished measurements. Sew 1 shoulder seam.

NECK EDGING

With RS facing, pick up and knit 67 (75, 75, 79, 83) sts along neck edge.

Work 3 rows in Seed st.
Bind off.

ASSEMBLY

Sew 2nd shoulder seam, including neck edging. Sew on sleeves between shoulder and last inc row on body. Sew side seams between top of curve and sleeves.

Sew pocket to the lower left front with the bottom edge 2 inches from the cast-on edge and the outside of the pocket 2 inches from the side seam. ■

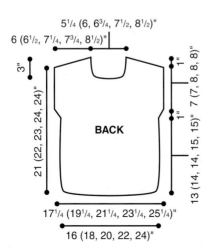

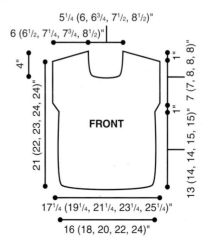

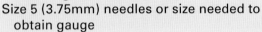

SLEEK & STYLISH SLEEVELESS TOP

DESIGN BY CECILY GLOWIK MACDONALD

WHAT'S IN THE BAG

NaturallyCaron.com Spa (DK weight; 75% microdenier acrylic/25% bamboo; 251 yds/85g per ball): 3 (3, 3, 4, 4) balls of green sheen #0004

Size 5 (3.75mm) needles or size needed to obtain gauge

3 LIGHT

SKILL LEVEL

■■□□ EASY

SIZES

Woman's small (medium, large, extra-large, 2X-large) Instructions are given for smallest size, with larger sizes in parentheses. When only 1 number is given, it applies to all sizes.

FINISHED MEASUREMENTS

Chest: 32 (36, 40, 44, 48) inches
Length: 18 inches

GAUGE

24 sts and 36 rows = 4 inches/10cm in Diagonal st.
To save time, take time to check gauge.

PATTERN STITCH

Diagonal Stitch
(multiple of 6 sts)
Row 1 (RS): *K5, p1; rep from * to end.
Row 2: P1, *k1, p5; rep from * to last 5 sts, k1, p4.
Row 3: K3, *p1, k5; rep from * to last 3 sts, p1, k2.
Row 4: P3, *k1, p5; rep from * to last 3 sts, k1, p2.

Row 5: K1, *p1, k5; rep from * to last 5 sts, p1, k4.
Row 6: *P5, k1; rep from * to end.
Rep Rows 1–6 for pat.

FRONT

Cast on 96 (108, 120, 132, 144) sts.
Work in garter st for ¾ inch, ending with a WS row.
Work in Diagonal St until piece measures 4 inches, ending with a WS row.
Work K3, P3 Rib until piece measures 7 inches, ending with a WS row.
Work in Diagonal St until piece measures 11 (10, 10, 9, 9) inches or desired length to armhole.

Armhole
Slipping the first st of every row pwise, continue in established pat until piece measures 16 inches, ending with a WS row.
Discontinue slipping

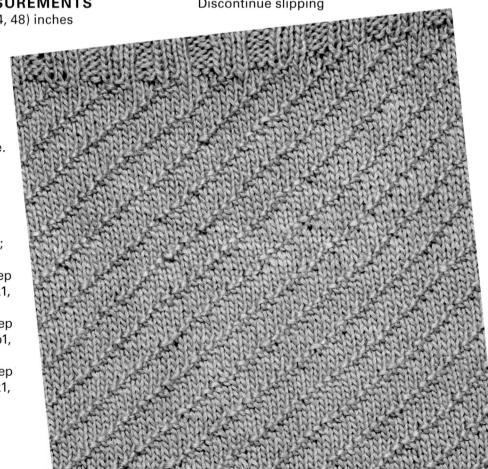

the first st; work K3, P3 Rib until piece measures 18 inches, ending with a WS row.
Bind off all sts in rib.

BACK

Work as for front, but work P3, K3 Rib at top 2 inches.

FINISHING

Block pieces to finished measurements, allowing waist ribbing to pull in naturally.

Starting at bottom, sew side seams for 11 (10, 10, 9, 9) inches, leaving rem 7 (8, 8, 9, 9) inches open for armholes. Beg at each shoulder edge, sew 3 (4, 5, 6, 7)-inch shoulder seams. Weave in ends. ■

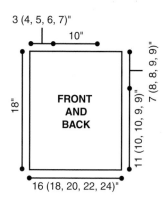

3 (4, 5, 6, 7)"

10"

18"

FRONT AND BACK

11 (10, 10, 9, 9)"

7 (8, 8, 9, 9)"

16 (18, 20, 22, 24)"

Tip Here's a great way to organize multiple projects in your knitting bag: place various projects in separate plastic containers with lids. When you're ready to work, just remove the top, and knit away! This keeps your projects and yarn neatly contained and avoids wasting precious time untangling yarn.

TAKE IT ON THE ROAD TANK

DESIGN BY DIANE ZANGL

WHAT'S IN THE BAG

Mission Falls 1824 Cotton
(worsted weight; 100% cotton;
85 yds/50g per ball): 6 (7, 8, 9)
balls vintage #775

Size 6 (4mm) needles or size needed to
obtain gauge
Size G/6 (4mm) crochet hook
Stitch holders
Stitch markers

SKILL LEVEL
■■□□ EASY

SIZES
Woman's small (medium, large, extra-
large) Instructions are given for smallest
size, with larger sizes in parentheses.
When only 1 number is given, it applies to
all sizes.

FINISHED MEASUREMENTS
Chest: 34 (36, 40, 47) inches
Length: 20 (20½, 22, 22½) inches

GAUGE
18 sts and 25 rows = 4 inches/10cm in K1,
P3 Rib.
To save time, take time to check gauge.

PATTERN STITCHES
K1, P1 Rib (odd number of sts)
Row 1 (RS): K1, *p1, k1; rep from * across.
Row 2: P1, *k1, p1; rep from * across.
  Rep Rows 1 and 2 for pat.

K1, P3 Rib (multiple of 4 sts + 1)
Row 1 (WS): P1, *k3, p1; rep from * across.
Row 2 (RS): K1, *p3, k1; rep from * across.
  Rep Rows 1 and 2 for pat.

BACK
Cast on 77 (81, 89, 101) sts.

Work in K1, P3 Rib until piece measures
13 (13, 14, 14) inches, ending with a WS row.

Shape underarm
Bind off 4 (4, 5, 7) sts at beg of next 2 rows—
69 (73, 79, 87) sts.
Dec row (RS): Ssk, work in pat to last 2 sts,
k2tog—67 (71, 77, 85) sts.
  Continue in established pat and rep Dec row
[every RS row] 3 (3, 4, 6) times—61 (65, 69,
73) sts.
  Work even until armhole measures 3 (3½,
4, 4½) inches, ending with a WS row.

Shape neck

Mark center 19 (23, 23, 23) sts.

Next row (RS): Work in K1, P1 Rib to first marker, join 2nd ball of yarn and bind off marked sts, work in K1, P1 Rib to end—21 (21, 23, 25) sts each side.

Working both sides at once with separate balls of yarn in established K1, P1 Rib, bind off 3 sts at each neck edge once, then 2 sts once—16 (16, 18, 20) sts each side.

Dec 1 st at each neck edge every RS row 3 (3, 3, 5) times—13 (13, 15, 15) sts each side.

Straps

Work even in established rib until armholes measure 7 (7½, 8, 8½) inches.

Bind off all sts.

FRONT

Work same as for back.

FINISHING

Weave in all ends. Block to finished measurements. Sew shoulder and side seams.

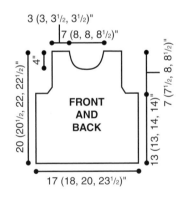

3 (3, 3½, 3½)"
7 (8, 8, 8½)"
4"
20 (20½, 22, 22½)"
FRONT AND BACK
13 (13, 14, 14)"
7 (7½, 8, 8½)"
17 (18, 20, 23½)"

Tip

If you don't want to be bothered with counting rows, purchase a row counter. String it onto a piece of colorful yarn, and wear it around your neck.

EDGINGS

Beg at underarm, work 1 row sc around entire armhole, keeping work flat; join with slip st and fasten off.

Rep for 2nd armhole.

Beg at shoulder seam, work 1 row sc around neckline.

Beg at side seam, work 1 row sc around lower edge. ■

"IT'S A WRAP" CABLED SHRUG

DESIGN BY COLLEEN SMITHERMAN

WHAT'S IN THE BAG

Nashua Creative Focus Worsted
(worsted weight; 75% wool/25%
alpaca; 220 yds/100g per ball): 4
(4, 5) skeins blue moor heather
#CFW.0791
Size 7 (4.5 mm) needles or size needed to
obtain gauge
Stitch markers
Stitch holder
Cable needle

SKILL LEVEL

■■■□ INTERMEDIATE

SIZES

Woman's small (medium, large) Instructions
are given for smallest size, with larger sizes in
parentheses. When only 1 number is given, it
applies to all sizes.

FINISHED MEASUREMENTS

Chest: 38 (42, 46) inches
Length to shoulder: 14½ (15¼, 15½) inches

GAUGE

19 sts and 25 rows = 4 inches/10cm in St st.
To save time, take time to check gauge.

SPECIAL ABBREVIATIONS

Cable 4 Back (C4B): Sl 2 to cn and hold in
back, k2, k2 from cn.
Cable 4 Front (C4F): Sl 2 to cn and hold in
front, k2, k2 from cn.
Make 1 (M1): Insert LH needle from front to
back under the running thread between the
last st worked and next st on RH needle; knit
into the back of resulting loop.

PATTERN STITCH

Braided Cable (10-st panel)
Row 1 (RS): P2, k6, p2.
Row 2 and all WS rows: K2, p6, k2.
Row 3: P2, k2, C4B, p2.

Row 5: Rep Row 1.
Row 7: P2, C4F, k2, p2.
Row 8: Rep Row 2.
Rep Rows 1–8 for pat.

PATTERN NOTES

A chart of the cable pattern is provided for
those preferring to work from charts.

Each front has a cable border; this border
is continued around the back neck by sewing
separate cable piece to back neck after back
is knit.

BACK

Cast on 90 (100, 110) sts.
Set up rib (RS): K2 (1, 2), work in P2, K2 Rib
to last 4 (3, 4) sts, p2, k2 (1, 2).

Continue in established rib until piece
measures 2 inches, ending with a WS row.

Beg working in St st and work even until
back measures 6½ (6¾, 6¾) inches, ending
with a WS row.

Shape armhole

Bind off 6 (7, 10) sts at beg of next 2 rows—
78 (86, 90) sts.

Work even until armhole measures 6¾ (7¼,
7½) inches, ending with a WS row.

Shape back neck & shoulders

Next row (RS): K20 (24, 25), join 2nd ball of
yarn and bind off center 38 (38, 40) sts, knit to
end of row.

Working both sides of neck with separate
balls of yarn, bind off 4 sts at each neck edge
once, then 2 sts once, then 1 st once; at the
same time, when armhole measures 8 (8½, 8¾)
inches, bind off 6 (8, 9) sts once, then 7 (9, 9)
sts once at each shoulder edge.

LEFT FRONT

Cast on 45 (50, 55) sts.
Set up rib and cable pat (RS): K1 (2, 3), *p2, k2;
rep from * 7 (8, 9) times, place marker, work
Braided Cable over next 10 sts, place marker,
k1, sl 1 wyif.
Row 2: P2, work Braided Cable between
markers, work established rib pat to end.

Rep Rows 1 and 2 until piece measures 2
inches, ending with a WS row.

Shape neck & armhole

Row 1 (RS): Knit to marker, work Braided Cable
between markers, k1, sl 1 wyif.
Row 2: P2, work Braided Cable between
markers, purl to end of row.
Dec row: Knit to 2 sts before first marker,
k2tog, work Braided Cable, k1, sl 1 wyif.

Continue in established pat and rep Dec row
[every 6 rows] 13 (13, 14) times and *at the same
time*, when the front measures 6½ (6¾, 6¾)
inches, ending with a WS row, shape armhole
as follows:
Next row (RS): Bind off 6 (7, 10) sts, work to
end of row.

Working in established pat, continue dec
at front neck, then work even until armhole

measures 8 (8½, 8¾) inches, ending with a
WS row.

Shape shoulder

At shoulder edge, bind off [6 (7, 8) sts] 3 times,
then [7 (8, 6) sts] once.

RIGHT FRONT

Cast on 45 (50, 55) sts.
Set up rib and cable pat (RS): Sl 1, k1, place
marker, work Braided Cable over next 10 sts,
place marker, *k2, p2; rep from * 7 (8, 9) times,
k1 (2, 3).
Row 2: Work established rib to marker, work
Braided Cable pat between markers, p2.

Rep Rows 1 and 2 until piece measures 2
inches, ending with a WS row.

Shape center front & armholes

Row 1 (RS): Sl 1, k1, work Braided Cable
between markers, knit to end of row.
Row 2: Purl to marker, work Braided Cable
between markers, p2.
Dec row (RS): Sl 1, k1, work Braided Cable, ssk,
knit to end of row.

Continue in established pat and rep Dec row
[every 6 rows] 13 (13, 14) times and *at the same
time*, when the front measures 6½ (6¾, 6¾)

Tip Here's a quick fix for less than ideal
lighting: Keep an inexpensive mini
LED headlamp in your knitting
bag. You can focus the light exactly
where you need it, and the light won't disturb
others nearby.

inches, ending with a RS row, shape armhole as follows:

Next row (WS): Bind off 6 (7, 10) sts, work to end of row.

Working in established pat, continue dec at front neck, then work even until armhole measures 8 (8½, 8¾) inches, ending with a RS row.

Shape shoulders

At shoulder edge, bind off [6 (7, 8) sts] 3 times, then [7 (8, 6) sts] once.

SLEEVES

Cast on 38 (46, 46) sts.

Set up rib and cable pat (RS): K2, [p2, k2] 3 (4, 4) times, place marker, work Braided Cable across next 10 sts, place marker, k2, [p2, k2] 3 (4, 4) times.

Continue in established pat, working Braided Cable between markers, until sleeve measures 2 inches, ending with a WS row.

Next row (RS): K14 (18, 18), work Braided Cable between markers, knit to end of row.

Working St st on either side of Braided Cable, work even until piece measures 3½ (3, 2½) inches, ending with a WS row.

Inc row (RS): K2, M1, work in pat to last 2 sts, M1, k2—40 (48, 48) sts.

Continue in pat and rep Inc row [every 5 (6, 6) rows] 19 (17, 18) times—76 (80, 82) sts.

Work even until sleeve measures 19½ (19¾, 20) inches, ending with a WS row.

Shape sleeve cap

Next 8 (12, 12) rows: Bind off 8 (6, 6) sts at beg of each row—12 (8, 10) sts.

Bind off rem sts.

Back neck cable

Cast on 14 sts.

Row 1 (RS): Sl 1, k1, work Braided Cable over next 10 sts, k2.

Row 2: P2, work Braided Cable, p2.

Rep Rows 1 and 2, allowing band to gently curl, until longer edge measures approx 13 (14, 14) inches. Place sts on holder.

FRONT TIES
Make 2

Cast on 10 sts.

Work in K2, P2 Rib until tie measures 9 inches.

FINISHING

Block all pieces to finished measurements. Sew long edge of back neck cable to back neck edge, easing in back neck fabric as necessary. If cable is too long, unravel extra rows, then bind off. Sew shoulder seems. Sew in sleeves. Sew sleeve and side seams. Sew ties to lower center fronts. Weave in all ends. ∎

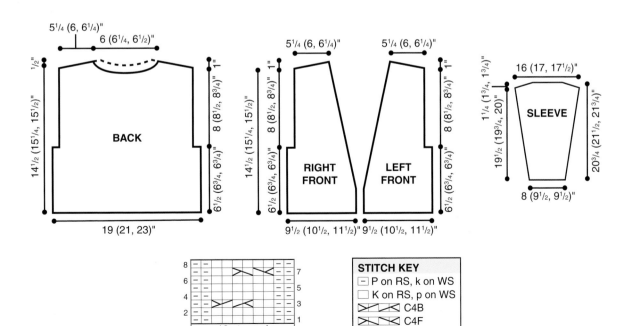

BRAIDED CABLE

STITCH KEY
- ⊟ P on RS, k on WS
- ☐ K on RS, p on WS
- ⟩⟨ C4B
- ⟩⟨ C4F

OUTBACK BASKET WEAVE PULLOVER

DESIGN BY MELISSA LEAPMAN

WHAT'S IN THE BAG

Schachenmayr Ecologico (worsted weight; 100% wool; 83 yds/50g per ball): 15 (16, 17, 18, 19, 20) balls medium gray #84

Size 8 (5mm) needles
Size 9 (5.5mm) needles or size needed to obtain gauge

SKILL LEVEL

■■■□ INTERMEDIATE

SIZES

Man's small (medium, large, extra-large, 2X-large, 3X-large) Instructions are given for smallest size, with larger sizes in parentheses. When only 1 number is given, it applies to all sizes.

FINISHED MEASUREMENTS

Chest: 45½ (48½, 51½, 54½, 57½, 60½) inches
Length: 26 (26½, 27, 27, 27½, 27½) inches

GAUGE

16 sts and 26 rows = 4 inches/10cm in Basket Weave pat with larger needles.
To save time, take time to check gauge.

PATTERN STITCHES

K3, P3 Rib (multiple of 6 sts + 3)
Row 1 (RS): K3, *p3, k3; rep from * to end.
Row 2: P3, *k3, p3; rep from * to end.
Rep Rows 1 and 2 for pat.

Basket Weave (multiple of 6 sts + 3)
Rows 1 and 3 (RS): P3, *k3, p3; rep from * to end.

Rows 2 and 4: K3, *p3, k3; rep from * to end.
Rows 5 and 7: K3, *p3, k3; rep from * to end.
Rows 6 and 8: P3, *k3, p3; rep from * to end.
Rep Rows 1–8 for pat.

Neckband Rib (multiple of 6 sts + 2)
Row 1 (RS): K1, *k3, p3; rep from * to last st, k1.
Row 2: P1, *k3, p3; rep from * to last st, p1.
Rep Rows 1 and 2 for pat.

PATTERN NOTE

For ease in finishing, one selvedge stitch has been added to each side; these stitches are not reflected in final measurements.

BACK

With smaller needles, cast on 93 (99, 105, 111, 117, 123) sts.

Work in K3, P3 Rib for 3 inches, ending with a WS row.

Change to larger needles and work even in Basket Weave pat until piece measures approx 15½ inches, ending with a WS row.

Shape armholes

Bind off 9 (12, 15, 15, 18, 18) sts at beg of next 2 rows—75 (75, 75, 81, 81, 87) sts.

Work even in established pat until armholes measure approx 9½ (10, 10½, 10½, 11, 11) inches, ending with a WS row.

Shape shoulders

Bind off 7 (7, 7, 8, 8, 9) sts at beg of next 4 rows, then bind off 8 (8, 8, 9, 9, 10) sts at beg of following 2 rows—31 sts.

Bind off.

FRONT

Work same as back until armholes measure 7¼ (7¾, 8¼, 8½, 8¾, 8¾) inches, ending with a WS row.

Shape neck

Work across first 30 (30, 30, 33, 33, 36) sts, join 2nd ball of yarn and bind off center 15 sts, work to end row.

Working both sides at once with separate balls of yarn, bind off 3 sts at each neck edge once, then 2 sts at each neck edge once—25 (25, 25, 28, 28, 31) sts each side.

Dec 1 st each neck edge [every row] twice, then dec 1 st each neck edge [every other row] once—22 (22, 22, 25, 25, 28) sts each side.

Work even until piece measures same as back to shoulders.

Tip What did we do before sticky notes? These nifty creations are our saving grace when it comes to knitting. Keep your place on your pattern by moving the sticky note down as you work— you'll never forget where you left off! Keep extra pads available in the glove compartment of your car and in your knitting bag.

Shape shoulders

Work same as for back.

SLEEVE

With smaller needles, cast on 39 (39, 39, 39, 45, 45) sts.

Work in K3, P3 Rib for 1½ inches, ending with a WS row.

Change to larger needles, beg Basket Weave pat, inc 1 st each side [every 4 rows] 1 (8, 16, 16, 14, 17) times, then [every 6 rows] 18 (13, 7, 7, 8, 5) times, working new sts into pat as they accumulate—77 (81, 85, 85, 89, 89) sts.

Work even until piece measures approx 21 (21½, 21½, 21½, 22, 21) inches, ending with a WS row.

Bind off.

FINISHING

Block pieces to finished measurements.
   Sew right shoulder seam.

NECKBAND

With RS facing and using smaller needles, pick up and knit 86 sts around neckline.

Work even in Neckband Rib Pat until band measures approx 2½ inches.

Bind off in rib.

ASSEMBLY

Sew left shoulder seam, including side of neckband. Fold neckband in half to WS and loosely whipstitch into place. Set in sleeves. Sew side seams. Weave in all ends. ■

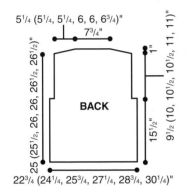

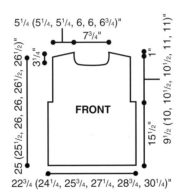

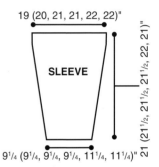

FOR THE LITTLE ONES

If you're searching for the perfect gift for next weekend's shower, you're in the right place! When it comes to knitting for those little cuties in your life, we've made it easier than ever to pack up your knitting bag for your excursions. With easy-to-memorize stitch combinations, you'll never lose your place again!

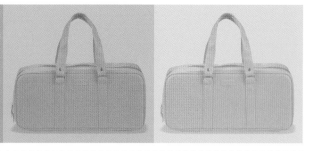

ROUNDABOUT RUFFLED TOP

DESIGN BY LOIS S. YOUNG

WHAT'S IN THE BAG

Reynolds Saucy (worsted weight; 100% cotton; 185 yds/100g per ball): 2 (3, 3, 4) balls coral reef #4545 (MC); 1 ball each persimmon #125 (A) and light yellow #133 (B)

Size 5 (3.75mm) straight and 16-inch circular needles or size needed to obtain gauge

Stitch markers, 1 in CC for beg of rnd

Stitch holders

SKILL LEVEL

 INTERMEDIATE

SIZES

Child's 2–4 (4–6, 6–8, 8–10)
Instructions are given for smallest size with larger sizes in parentheses. When only 1 number is given, it applies to all sizes.

FINISHED MEASUREMENTS

Chest: 24 (26, 28, 30) inches
Length to shoulder: 13 (14¼, 17¼, 19¼) inches

GAUGE

20 sts and 28 rows = 4 inches/10cm in St st.
To save time, take time to check gauge.

SPECIAL ABBREVIATIONS

Place marker (pm): Place a marker on needle to separate sections.
Centered Double Decrease (S2KP2): Slip 2 sts kwise, k1, pass slipped sts over.

BACK

With A, cast on 64 (70, 74, 80) sts.

Knit 1 row.
Change to MC and knit 6 rows.
Work in St st until back measures 7½ (8¼, 10¼, 11¾) inches, ending with a WS row.

Shape armholes

Bind off 4 (4, 4, 5) sts at beg of next 2 rows, and 3 sts at beg of the following 2 rows—50 (56, 60, 64) sts.
Dec row (RS): K1, ssk, knit to last 3 sts, k2tog, k1—48 (54, 58, 62) sts.
Rep Dec row [every RS row] 0 (0, 0, 1) time more—48 (54, 58, 60) sts.
Work even until armhole measures 2½ (3, 3½, 4) inches, ending with a WS row.

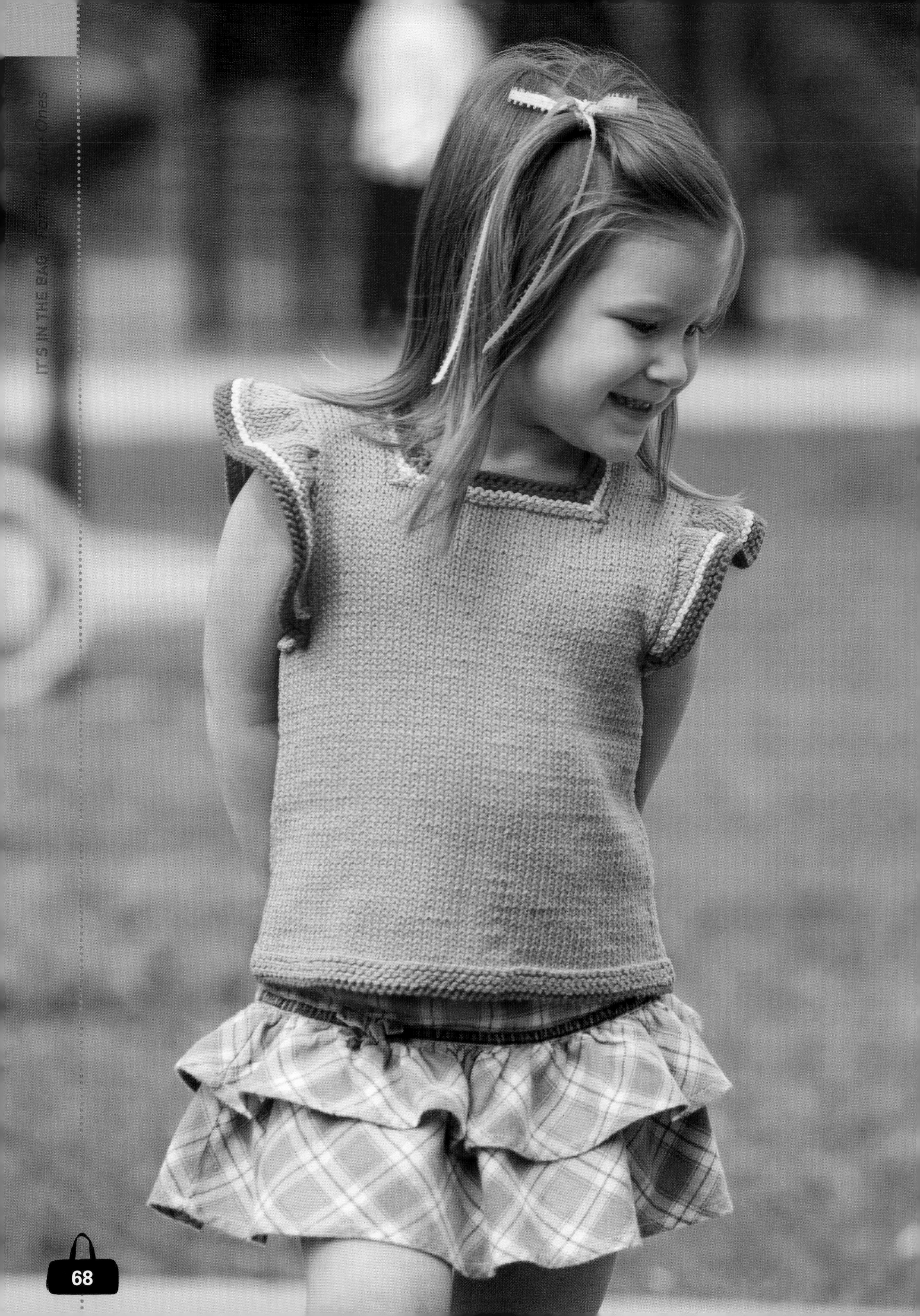

Divide for neck

Next row (RS): K12 (14, 15, 16) sts for left shoulder, join 2nd ball of yarn and k24 (26, 28, 28) sts and put on holder for neck, k12 (14, 15, 16) sts for right shoulder.

Working both sides at once, work even until armholes measure 5 ½ inches, ending with a WS row.

Shape shoulders

Bind off 6 (7, 8, 8) sts at armhole edges at beg of next 2 rows and 6 (7, 7, 8) sts at beg of following 2 rows.

FRONT

Work same as for back.

ASSEMBLY

Sew shoulder and side seams.

NECK BORDER

With RS facing, using circular needle and MC, beg at right shoulder, pick up and knit 16 (16, 18, 18) sts evenly spaced along right yoke; pm, k24 (26, 28, 28) sts from back neck holder; pm, pick up and knit 32 (32, 36, 36) sts along left yoke; pm, k24 (26, 28, 28) sts from front neck holder; pm, pick up and knit 16 (16, 18, 18) sts along right yoke; place beg of rnd marker—112 (116, 128, 128) sts.

Rnds 1, 3, 5: Purl with color used on previous rnd.

Rnd 2 (dec): With B, *knit to 1 st before marker, sl 1, remove marker, return slipped st to LH needle, replace marker on RH needle, S2KP2, knit to 2 sts before marker, slip both sts, remove marker, S2KP2, replace marker; rep

from * once more, knit to end—104 (108, 120, 120) sts.

Rnds 4 and 6: With A, work as for Rnd 2—88 (92, 104, 104) sts.

Rnd 7: Bind off pwise.

UNDERARM BORDER

With RS facing, using circular needle and MC, pick up and knit 16 (16, 16, 18) sts along bottom of armhole. Turn and bind off kwise.

RUFFLE

Count up 22 (26, 32, 36) rows from underarm and mark positions on front and back.

With RS facing, using circular needle and MC, beg at first marker, pick up and knit around upper armhole at rate of 3 sts for every 2 rows as follows: *pick up and knit 1 st, yo, pick up and knit 1 st; rep from *, ending at 2nd marker—approx 51 (59, 71, 79) sts.

Work back and forth in St st and at end of each row, [pick up and knit (on RS)/purl (on WS) 6 more sts along armhole] 6 (6, 8, 12) times, [(RS) pick up and knit or (WS) purl 4 more sts along armhole] 2 (4, 4, 0) times—approx 95 (111, 135, 151) sts; exact st count is not critical.

Knit next WS row.
Change to B and knit 2 rows.
Change to A and knit 3 rows.
Bind off kwise on WS.

FINISHING

Sew ends of ruffle to underarm.

Weave in ends. Block to finished measurements. ■

Tip No stitch marker? No problem! Using a contrasting-color yarn, make a slip knot as if to cast on one stitch. Cut about a ½ inch below the knot, and voilà—a stitch marker!

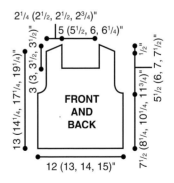

2¼ (2½, 2½, 2¾)"

5 (5½, 6, 6¼)"

3 (3, 3½, 3½)"

13 (14¼, 17¼, 19¼)"

½"

5½ (6, 7, 7½)"

FRONT AND BACK

7½ (8¼, 10¼, 11¾)"

12 (13, 14, 15)"

LITTLE PRINCESS DRESS UP SET

DESIGNS BY LOIS S. YOUNG

WHAT'S IN THE BAG

Berroco Plush (bulky weight; 100% nylon; 90 yds/50g per skein): 1 (1, 2) skeins raspberry strawberry #1926 (MC)

Berroco Touché (worsted weight; 50% cotton/50% rayon; 89 yds/50g per hank): 1 hank sachet #7931 (CC)

Size 10 (6mm) 24- or 29-inch circular needle or size needed to obtain gauge

SKILL LEVEL

 ■■□□ EASY

SIZES

Child's 2 (4–6, 8) Instructions are given for smallest size with larger sizes in parentheses. When only 1 number is given, it applies to all sizes.

"MINK" STOLE

FINISHED MEASUREMENTS

Length: 32 (36, 40) inches
Width: 4 (5, 6) inches

GAUGE

12 sts and 24 rows = 4 inches/10cm in garter st with MC. To save time, take time to check gauge.

STOLE

With MC, cast on 106 (120, 134) sts.
  Knit 5 (6, 7) rows.
  With CC, knit 1 row, purl 1 row.
  With MC, knit 4 (6, 8) rows.

Rep [last 6 (8, 10) rows] 3 more times.
With MC, knit 1 row.
With MC, bind off kwise on WS.

CROWN

WHAT'S IN THE BAG

Berroco Touché (worsted weight; 50% cotton/50% rayon; 89 yds/50g per hank): 1 hank sachet #7931 (CC)

Berroco Lumina (worsted weight; 54% cotton/36% acrylic/10% polyester; 95 yds/25g per hank): 1 hank lip gloss #1607 (CC)

Size 7 (4.5mm) straight and double-pointed (set of 2) needles or size needed to obtain gauge

FINISHED MEASUREMENTS

Circumference (will stretch when worn): 16½ (18, 20½) inches
Height: 3½ (4, 4½) inches

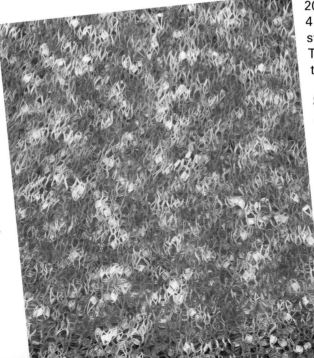

GAUGE

20 sts and 40 rows = 4 inches/10cm in garter stitch with MC. To save time, take time to check gauge.

SPECIAL ABBREVIATION

Make 1 (M1): Insert LH needle from front to back under the running thread between the last st worked and next st on RH needle; knit into the back of resulting loop.

SPECIAL TECHNIQUES

Attached I-cord: Without turning, slide sts to other end of needle. K2, ssk, pick up and knit 1 st from edge.

Unattached I-cord Row: Without turning, slide sts to other end of needle, k3.

PATTERN NOTE

Top and bottom of point will occur on different-side rows on different sizes. When changing from one to another, always work increases and decreases at point edge of crown.

CROWN

With MC, cast on 11 (13, 15) sts.
 Mark beg of RS row.

Bottom to top of point

RS rows: Knit to last st, M1, k1—1 st inc.
WS rows: K1, M1, knit to end—1 st inc.
 Work RS and WS rows until there are 19 (23, 27) sts in row.
 Knit 1 row.

Top to bottom of point

RS rows: Knit to last 3 sts, k2tog, k1—1 st dec.
WS rows: K1, ssk, knit to end of row—1 st dec.
 Work RS and WS rows until there are 11 (13, 15) sts in row.
 Knit 1 row.
 1 point complete.
 Make 5 more points in same manner.
 Bind off.
 Sew ends of crown tog.

BOTTOM I-CORD BORDER

With dpns and CC, cast on 3 sts.
 With RS facing, pick up and knit 1 st from bottom of crown.
 Work Attached I-cord around bottom of crown at rate of 1 row per ridge of garter st.
 When border is complete, bind off.
 Sew ends of I-cord tog.

POINT I-CORD BORDER

Beg border several ridges up from bottom of one point.
 Work as for bottom border, working attached I-cord up point at rate of 1 row per ridge, ending 1 row before point.
Turning the point: Work 2 rows Attached I-cord in next st; work 1 row Attached I-cord in point, but omit the "pick up and knit 1 st"; work 1 row Unattached I-cord; work 1 row Unattached I-cord, but pick up and knit 1 st in point st; work 2 rows Attached I-cord in next st (point completed).

Work Attached I-cord down point to bottom st between points; skip this st and begin next point's border.

Continue around points.

Bind off when border is complete, sew ends of I-cord tog.

BALLET LENGTH SKIRT

WHAT'S IN THE BAG

Plymouth Eros (worsted weight; 100% nylon; 165 yds/50g per ball): 2 (2, 3) balls red/pink #2010 (MC)

Plymouth Encore DK (DK weight; 75% acrylic/25% wool; 150 yds/50g per ball): 1 ball fuchsia #1385 (CC)

Size 5 (3.75mm) needles

Size 9 (5.5mm) double-point needles (set of 2)

Size 11 (6mm) 24 or 29-inch circular needle or size needed to obtain gauge

Stitch marker

FINISHED MEASUREMENTS

Length: 12 (14, 17) inches
Waist: 21 (23, 25) inches, before gathering with tie

GAUGE

13 sts and 16 rows = 4 inches/10cm in St st. To save time, take time to check gauge.

WAISTBAND

Using smaller needles and CC, cast on 8 sts. Knit 2 rows.
Row 1 (eyelet row, RS): K2, k2tog, [yo] twice, ssk, k2.
Row 2: K3, [k1, p1] in double-yo, k3.
Rows 3 and 5: Knit.
Rows 4 and 6: K2, p4, k2.
Rep [Rows 1–6] 21 (23, 25) times.
Knit 2 rows.
Bind off kwise on WS.

SKIRT

With RS facing, using larger needle and MC, pick up and knit along edge at rate of 3 sts for every 4 rows (approx 134, 143, 152 sts); place marker for beg of rnd.

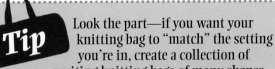

Tip Look the part—if you want your knitting bag to "match" the setting you're in, create a collection of exciting knitting bags of many shapes and sizes. Scatter your bags decoratively around the house, each equipped with a project ready to go. When it's time to leave for your outing, pick the bag that suits your style!

Knit all rnds until skirt measures 11 (13, 16) inches.

With MC and CC held tog, knit 1 rnd, purl 1 rnd, knit 1 rnd.

Bind off loosely pwise.

Weave in ends. Block.

WAISTBAND TIE

Using dpns and 1 strand each MC and CC held tog, cast on 4 sts; do not turn.
I-cord row: Slide sts to other end of needle, k4, do not turn.
Rep I-cord row until tie measures 32 (36, 40) inches.
Bind off.
Weave in ends.
Thread tie through holes on waistband. Tack tie to waistband in center of skirt to prevent it from being pulled out. ■

BODACIOUS BOBBLE HAT

DESIGN BY IRINA POLUDNENKO

WHAT'S IN THE BAG

Tahki Stacy Charles Torino (worsted weight; 100% merino wool; 94 yds/50g per ball): 1 ball each lime green #119 (A), fuchsia #120 (B) and dark lavender #129 (C)

4 MEDIUM

Size 8 (5mm) double-pointed (set of 5) and 16-inch circular needles or size needed to obtain gauge
Size F/5 (3.75mm) crochet hook
Stitch markers (1 in CC for beg of rnd)

SKILL LEVEL
 EASY

SIZES
Child's small (medium, large)

FINISHED MEASUREMENT
Circumference: 16 (17¾, 19½) inches

GAUGE
18 sts and 32 rnds = 4 inches/10cm in pat st.
To save time, take time to check gauge.

PATTERN STITCH
Stripe pat (any number of sts)
Rnd 1: With A, knit.
Rnd 2: With A, purl.
Rnds 3 and 4: With B, knit.
Rnds 5 and 6: Rep Rnds 1 and 2.
Rnds 7 and 8: With C, knit.
    Rep Rnds 1–8 for Stripe pat.

PATTERN NOTES
When working Stripe pattern, carry colors not in use up inside of hat.

    Change to double-pointed needles when stitches no longer fit comfortably on circular needle.

HAT
With A, cast on 72 (80, 88) sts; place marker for beg of rnd and join, taking care not to twist sts. Beg with Rnd 2, work [Rnds 1–8 of Stripe pat] 5 (6, 7) times, then work Rnds 1 and 2 once more.

Next rnd: Continuing in Stripe pat, *k9 (10, 11), place marker; rep from * around.
Dec rnd: Knit to 2 sts before marker, k2tog; rep from * around—64 (72, 80) sts.

    Continue in Stripe pat and rep Dec rnd [every 4th rnd] 7 (8, 9) times—8 sts rem.

    Work 14 more rnds in Stripe pat.

    With A, bind off.

    Weave in all ends.

BOBBLE TASSELS
Make 8
With B, cast on 3 sts.
Row 1: K1, [k1, yo, k1, yo, k1] in next st, k1—7 sts.
Row 2: Purl.
Row 3: Knit.
Row 4: Purl.
Row 5: K1, ssk, k1, k2tog, k1—5 sts.
Row 6: K1, p3tog, k1—3 sts.
Row 7: K3tog and put resulting st on crochet hook.

    Cut yarn, leaving a 5-inch tail.

    With crochet hook and A, beg with the last st of bobble, chain 20 sts, attach with slip st to a bound-off st on hat, turn; work a slip st in each chain st, cut yarn and fasten off.

    Using 5-inch tail and tapestry needle, draw through edge sts to form bobble.

    Weave all ends inside bobble.

    Make 7 more bobble tassels with 3 bobbles in B and 4 bobbles in C; work all tassel cords in A and attach each one to next bound-off st on top of hat. Make tassel cords different lengths as desired. ∎

Tip Always have your scissors handy by tying them onto a pretty piece of ribbon. You can attach them to your yarn bag or wear them around your neck.

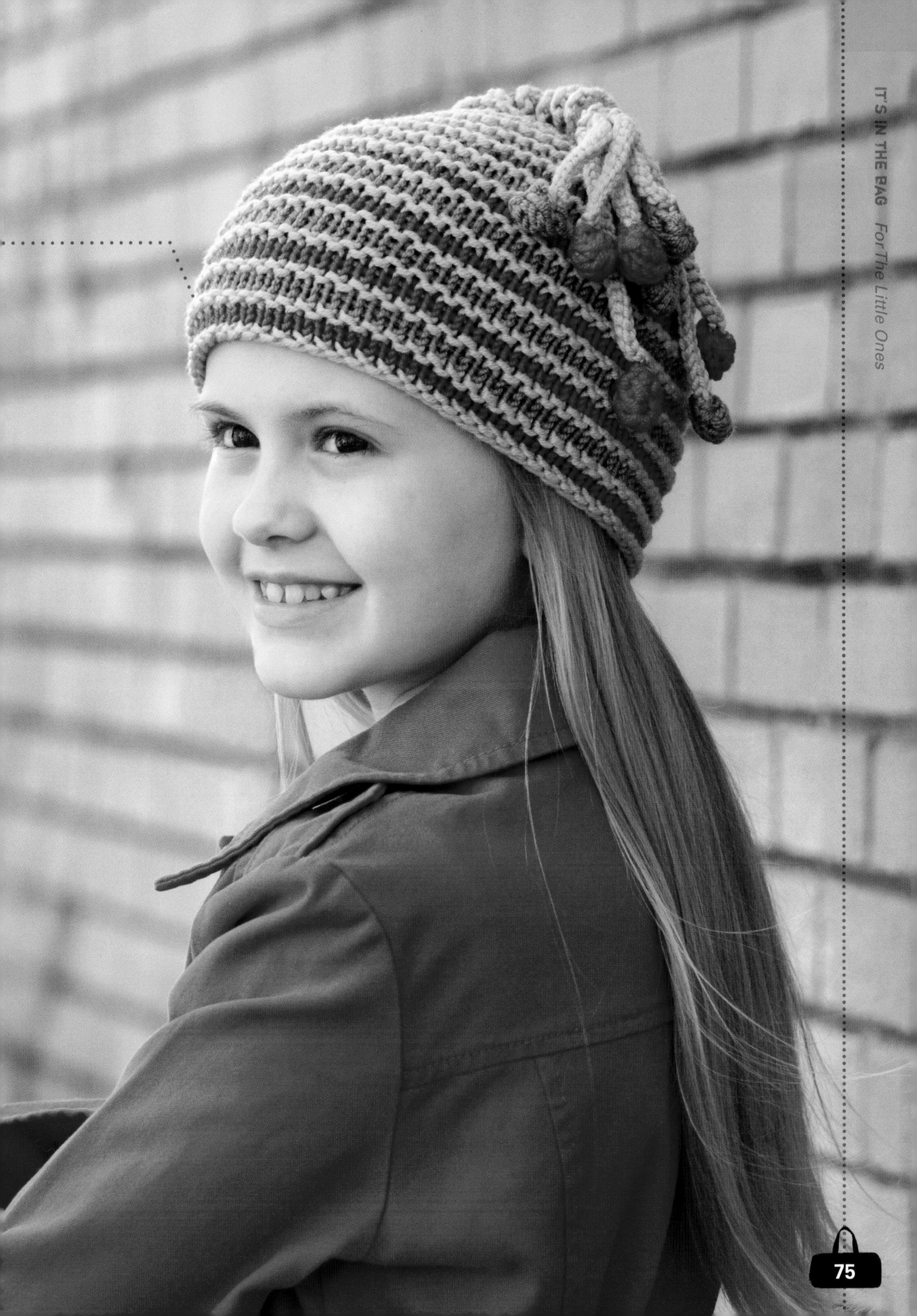

LACY A-LINE BABY DRESS

DESIGN BY SHIRLEY MACNULTY

WHAT'S IN THE BAG

Rowan Cashsoft Baby DK
   (DK weight; 57% extra
   fine merino/33% acrylic
   microfiber/10% cashmere; 142
   yds/50g per ball): 4 balls bloom #00815

3 LIGHT

Size 6 (4mm) straight and 16-inch circular
   needles or size needed to obtain gauge
1 [½-inch] button to match yarn
Small amount sewing thread to match
   button color
Sewing needle

SKILL LEVEL

■■■□ INTERMEDIATE

SIZES

Infant's 6–9 (9–12, 12–18) months Instructions
are given for the smallest size; with larger sizes
in parentheses. When only 1 number is given,
it applies to all sizes.

FINISHED MEASUREMENTS

Chest: 18½ (20½, 22½) inches
Length to shoulders: 12¾ (13½, 14¾) inches

GAUGE

23 sts and 32 rows = 4 inches/10cm in Lacy pat.
To save time, take time to check gauge.

SPECIAL ABBREVIATION

Make 1 (M1): Insert LH needle from front to
back under the running thread between the
last st worked and next st on RH needle; knit
into the back of resulting loop.

PATTERN STITCH

Lace Pat for Back/Front [multiple of 14 (16, 18)
sts +13]
Row 1 (RS): K4, *k2tog, yo, k1, yo, ssk, k9 (11,
13); rep from * to last 9 sts, k2tog, yo, k1, yo,
ssk, k4.
Row 2: and all WS rows: Purl.
Row 3: K3, *k2tog, yo, k3, yo, ssk, k7 (9, 11);

rep from * to last 10 sts, k2tog, yo, k3, ssk, k3.
Row 5: K4, *yo, ssk, yo, k3tog, yo, k9 (11, 13); rep
from * to last 9 sts, yo, ssk, yo, k3tog, yo, k4.
Row 7: K5, *yo, sk2p, yo, k11 (13, 15); rep from
* to last 8 sts, yo, sk2p, yo, k5
Row 9: K11 (12, 13), *k2tog, yo, k1, yo, ssk, k9
(11, 13); rep from * to last 2 (1, 0) sts, k2 (1, 0).
Row 11: K10 (11, 12), *k2tog, yo, k3, yo, ssk, k7
(9, 11); rep from * to last 3 (2, 1) sts, k3 (2, 1).
Row 13: K11 (12, 13), *yo, ssk, yo, k3tog, yo, k9
(11, 13); rep from * to last 2 (1, 0) sts, k2 (1, 0).
Row 15: K12 (13, 14), *yo, sk2p, yo, k11 (13, 15);
rep from * to last 15 (16, 17) sts, sk2p, yo, k12
(13, 14).
Row 16: Purl.
   Rep Rows 1–16 for pat.

Lace Pat for Sleeves
*Note: The number of knit sts at beg and end of
rows will inc twice as the sleeve inc are made.*
Row 1 (RS): K3 (4, 3), [k2tog, yo, k1, yo, ssk, k9
(9, 11)] twice, k2tog, yo, k1, ssk, k3 (4, 3).
Row 2 and all WS rows: Purl.
Row 3: K2 (3, 2), [k2tog, yo, k3, yo, ssk, k7 (7, 9)]
twice, k2tog, yo, k3, yo, ssk, k2 (3, 2).
Row 5: K3 (4, 3), [yo, ssk, yo, k3tog, yo, k9 (9,
11)] twice, yo, ssk, yo, k3tog, yo, k3 (4, 3).
Row 7: K4 (5, 4), [yo, sk2p, yo, k11 (11, 13)]
twice, yo, sk2p, yo, k4 (5, 4).
Row 9: K1, M1, k9 (10, 10), k2tog, yo, k1, yo,
ssk, k9 (9, 11), k2tog, yo, k1, yo, ssk, k9 (10, 10),
M1, k1.

   *Note: The M1 inc is worked on just this first
round of the sleeve pat rep and is shown here.
The 2nd M1 inc is worked on Row 1 of the first
rep. To keep in pat after the incs, the number of
knit sts at the beg and end of the rows is also
increased.*
Row 11: K10 (11, 11), k2tog, yo, k3, yo, ssk, k7
(7, 9), k2tog, yo, k3, yo, ssk, k10 (11, 11).
Row 13: K11 (12, 12), yo, ssk, yo, k3tog, yo, k9
(9, 11), yo, ssk, yo, k3tog, yo, k11 (12, 12).
Row 15: K12 (13, 13), yo, sk2p, yo, k11 (11, 13),
yo sk2p, yo, k12 (13, 13).
Row 16: Purl.
   Rep Rows 1–16 for pat, increasing again on
the first Row 1 rep.

PATTERN NOTES

A chart is provided for the Lace pattern (front/back) for those preferring to work from charts.

When decreasing or increasing, be sure that if you work a pattern stitch yarn over that you also work a corresponding pattern stitch decrease, and if you work a pattern stitch decrease that you have a corresponding pattern stitch yarn over or your stitch count will not come out even. Do not confuse decrease shaping stitches with pattern stitches.

The back neck is split and closed with a button.

The garter stitch bottom edge is a slightly wider gauge than the pattern stitch; when blocking, the bottom should be wider than the chest (see schematic).

BACK

Using long-tail method, cast on 55 (61, 67) sts.

Knit 4 rows.

Purl 1 row.

Work even in Lace pat until piece measures 9 (9½, 10) inches or desired length to underarm.

Shape Armholes

Continuing in pat, bind off 3 (4, 4) sts at the beg of the next 2 rows—49 (53, 59) sts.

Dec row (RS): K2, ssk, work in pat to last 3 sts, k2tog, k1—47 (51, 57) sts.

Rep Dec row [every RS row] 2 (2, 3) times more—43 (47, 51) sts.

Work even until armhole measures 2¾ (3, 3¾) inches, ending with a WS row,

RIGHT BACK

Row 1 (RS): Work 21 (23, 25) sts; turn, leaving rem 22 (24, 26) sts on holder.

Row 2: Cast on 3 sts, k3 (the sts just cast-on), purl to end—24 (26, 28) sts.

Next 6 rows: Work 21 (23, 25) sts in established Lace pat and 3 new sts in garter st.

Shape Right Back Shoulder

Bind off 3 (4, 4) sts at beg of next row, then 4 (5, 5) at the beg of the next 2 RS rows. Bind off rem 13 (12, 14) sts.

LEFT BACK

Row 1 (RS): Slip sts back to needle, join yarn and work to end of row.

Row 2: Purl to last st, k1.

Next 7 rows: Rep last 2 rows, ending with Row 1.

Shape Left Back Shoulder

Bind off 3 (4, 4) sts at beg of next row, then 4 (5, 5) sts at the beg of next 2 WS rows.

Note: *At some point in this section, you will work a yo for the Lace pat near the right edge that can be used for the buttonhole.*

Bind off the rem 11 (10, 12) sts.

FRONT

Work front the same as back until piece measures 1 (1, 1¼) inches less than back to shoulders.

Shape Front Neck

Work in pat across 16 (18, 20) sts, join a 2nd ball of yarn and bind off center 11 sts, work in pat to end of row—16 (18, 20) sts each side.

Working both sides at once with separate balls of yarn, bind off 2 sts at each neck edge once, then dec 1 st at each neck edge on RS rows 3 (2, 4) times—11 (14, 14) sts each side.

Work even in pat until front measures same as for back to shoulders, ending with a WS row.

Bind off 3 (4, 4) sts at beg of the next 2 rows, then 4 (5, 5) sts at beg of the next 4 rows.

SLEEVES

With long-tail method, cast on 39 (41, 43) sts.

Tip Make waiting in line worthwhile! Choose a bag that rests comfortably across your chest and shoulder, allowing for easy maneuvering of your project and yarn.

Knit 4 rows.

Purl 1 row.

Work 18 (20, 24) rows in Lace Sleeve pat, inc as indicated in the pat—43 (45, 47) sts.

Sleeve Cap

Bind off 3 (4, 4) sts at beg of the next 2 rows—37 (37, 39) sts.

Dec row (RS): K1, ssk, work in pat to last 3 sts, k2tog, k1—35 (35, 37) sts.

Rep Dec rows [every RS row] 10 (10, 11) times—15 sts.

Bind off.

FINISHING

Sew shoulder seams. Overlap right back neck with left back neck and sew closed at bottom.

NECKLINE

With circular needle, beg at the left neck edge, pick up and knit 11 (10, 12) left back neck sts, 15 (16, 17) left front sts, 11 front sts, 15 (16, 17) right front sts, and 13 (12, 14) right back neck sts—65 (65, 71) sts.

Knit 3 rows. Bind off loosely kwise.

ASSEMBLY

Set in sleeves. Sew side and sleeve seams. Weave in loose ends. Block to finished measurements. Sew button on right back neck edge to correspond to the pattern yo on left neck edge. ■

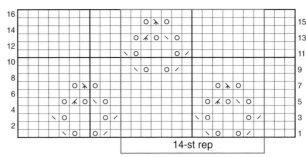

LACE PATTERN FRONT/BACK (SIZE 6-9)

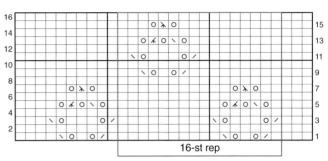

LACE PATTERN FRONT/BACK (SIZE 9-12)

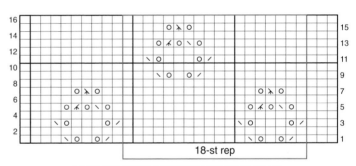

LACE PATTERN FRONT/BACK (SIZE 12-18)

STITCH KEY
- ☐ K on RS, p on WS
- ☑ K2tog
- ⊙ Yo
- ◹ Ssk
- ⊀ K3tog
- ⋏ Sk2p

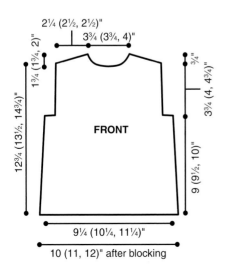

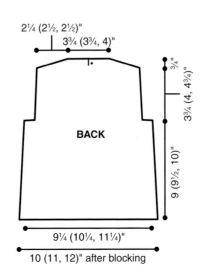

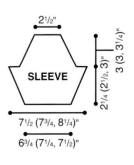

BABY DEAREST

DESIGNS BY KATHARINE HUNT

WHAT'S IN THE BAG

Plymouth Jeannee D.K. (DK weight; 51% cotton/49% acrylic; 136 yds/50g per ball): 3 (4, 4) balls pale blue #21 (A) and 4 (5, 6) balls denim #10 (B)

Size 3 (3.25mm) 16-inch circular needle (hat)
Size 4 (3.5mm) needles (sweater)
Size 5 (3.75mm) double-point and 16-inch circular needle or size needed to obtain gauge (hat)
Size 6 (4mm) needles or size needed to obtain gauge (sweater)
Size G/6 (4mm) crochet hook (optional)
Stitch markers, 1 in CC for beg of rnd
3 (3, 4) [15mm] buttons

SKILL LEVEL

 ▪▪▪▷ EXPERIENCED

SIZES

Sweater: Child's 2 (4, 6) Instructions are given for smallest size, with larger sizes in parentheses. When only 1 number is given, it applies to all sizes.
Hat: Child's small (medium/large)

FINISHED MEASUREMENTS

Chest: 27 (31½, 36) inches
Length to shoulders: 14 (16, 17¾) inches
Hat circumference: 16 (18) inches

GAUGE

Sweater: 22 sts and 39 rows = 4 inches/10cm in Honeycomb pat st with size 6 needles.
Hat: 24 sts and 41 rnds = 4 inches/10cm in Honeycomb pat with size 5 needles.
To save time, take time to check gauge.

SPECIAL ABBREVIATIONS

Make Bobble (MB): [K1, p1] 3 times, all into the next st, then pass last 5 sts over the first st and off the needle.

Place marker (pm): Place marker on needle to separate patterns.
Yarn forward (yf): Bring yarn between needles to front of work.
Yarn back (yb): Bring yarn between needles to back of work.

PATTERN STITCHES

Honeycomb Pat (worked flat on multiple of 12 sts + 15)

Sts should only be counted on Rows 1, 6, 7 and 12; if counting on other rows, do not count the yo's and resulting sts on following rows.
Row 1 (WS): With A, knit.
Row 2 (RS): With B, k6, *[sl 1, yo] twice, sl 1, k9; rep from *, ending last rep k6.
   Note: Be sure to keep the 2 yo's carefully positioned between the 3 slipped sts.
Row 3: With B, p6, *sl 1, purl the first yo, sl 1, knit the next yo, sl 1, p9; rep from *, ending last rep p6.
   Note: Slip each A slipped st onto RH needle before working the following yo.
Row 4: With B, k6, *[sl 1, k1] twice, sl 1, k9; rep from *, ending last rep k6.
Row 5: With B, p6, *[sl 1, p1] twice, sl 1, p9; rep from *, ending last rep p6.
Row 6: With A, k5, *k2tog, k3, ssk, k7; rep from *, ending last rep k5.
Row 7: With A, knit.
Row 8: With B, k1, sl 1, yo, sl 1, *k9, [sl 1, yo] twice, sl 1; rep from * to last 12 sts, k9, sl 1, yo, sl 1, k1.
Row 9: With B, [p1, sl 1] twice, *p9, sl 1, purl the first yo, sl 1, knit the next yo, sl 1; rep from * to last 13 sts, p9, [sl 1, p1] twice.
Row 10: With B, [k1, sl 1] twice, *k9, [sl 1, k1] twice, sl 1; rep from * to last 13 sts, k9, [sl 1, k1] twice.
Row 11: With B, [p1, sl 1] twice, *p9, [sl 1, p1] twice, sl 1; rep from * to last 13 sts, p9, [sl 1, p1] twice.
Row 12: With A, k3, *ssk, k7, k2tog, k3; rep from * to end.
   Rep Rows 1–12 for pat.

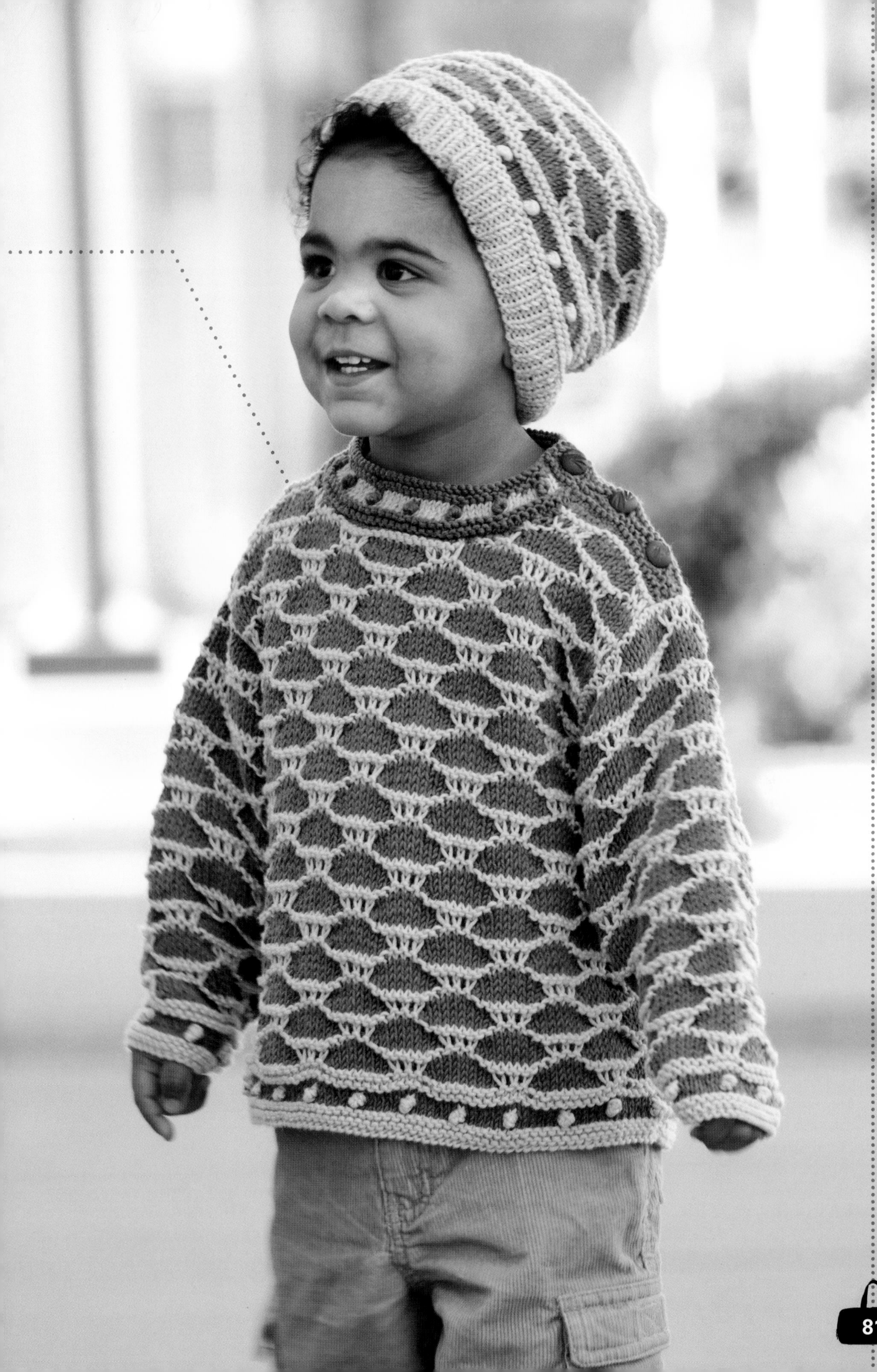

Honeycomb Pat (worked in round on multiple of 12 sts)

Sts should only be counted on Rnds 1, 6, 7 and 12; if counting on other rnds, do not count the yo's and resulting sts on following rnds.

Rnd 1: With A, purl.

Rnd 2: With B, *k2, [sl 1, yo] twice, sl 1, k7; rep from * around.

Note: Be sure to keep the 2 yo's carefully positioned between the 3 slipped sts.

Rnd 3: With B, *k2, sl 1, knit the first yo, sl 1, purl the next yo, sl 1, k7; rep from * around.

Note: Slip each A slipped st onto RH needle before working the following yo.

Rnds 4 and 5: With B, *k2, [sl 1, k1] twice, sl 1, k7; rep from * around.

Rnd 6: With A, *k1, k2tog, k3, ssk, k6; rep from * around.

Rnd 7: With A, purl.

Rnd 8: With B, *k8, [sl 1, yo] twice, sl 1, k1; rep from * around.

Rnd 9: With B, *k8, sl 1, knit the first yo, sl 1, purl the next yo, sl 1, k1; rep from * around.

Rnds 10 and 11: With B, *k8, [k1, sl 1] twice, sl 1, k1; rep from * around.

Rnd 12: With A, *k1, *k2tog, k3, ssk, k6; rep from *around.

Rep Rnds 1–12 for pat.

Stripe Pattern

Rnd 1: With A, knit.

Rnd 2: With A, purl.

Rnds 3–6: With B, knit.

Rep Rnds 1–6 for pat.

SPECIAL TECHNIQUE

1-Row 3-St Buttonhole: Work to buttonhole position, yf, slip next st pwise, yb; [slip next st, then pass 2nd st on RH needle over first st and off RH needle] 3 times to bind off 3 sts; slip first st on RH needle back to LH needle; turn. Wyib, cable cast on 4 sts (1 more than bound off) as follows: insert RH needle between the first and 2nd sts on LH needle, draw up a loop, and place it on the LH needle; rep from * 3 times; turn. Wyib, slip first st on LH needle to RH needle and pass the extra cast-on st over it to close the buttonhole. (This 4th st worked and is not part of the 3-St Buttonhole).

PATTERN NOTES

In order to maintain the correct stitch count when shaping armholes, neck and shoulders,

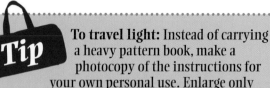

To travel light: Instead of carrying a heavy pattern book, make a photocopy of the instructions for your own personal use. Enlarge only the part you're working on, making it easier to keep track of your progress.

unless shaping on rows with the original number of stitches (i.e., Rows 1, 6, 7 and 12), omit yarn overs immediately following or before the edges that will be affected by the shaping. (Work the yarn overs on the rest of that row as required by the pattern stitch.)

When working Honeycomb pattern, count stitches on Rows 1, 6, 7 and 12; if counting on other rows, do not count the yarn overs or their resulting stitches.

Pattern is written as shown on a boy with button band on left shoulder; if preferred for a girl, reverse it to the right shoulder.

For hat, change to double-point needles when stitches no longer fit comfortably on circular needle.

SWEATER

BACK

With larger needles and A, cast on 75 (87, 99) sts.

Knit 4 rows.

Change to B and work 2 rows St st.

Bobble row (RS): K1 B, *MB with A, k5 B; rep from * to last 2 sts, MB with A, k1 B.

Cut A.

With B, purl 1 row.

With A, knit 3 rows.

Beg Honeycomb pat and work even until piece measures approx 7¾ (9½, 10½) inches, ending with Row 1 or 7 of pat.

Armhole

Bind off 6 sts at the beg of the next 2 rows, omitting yo's at edges if necessary to maintain st count—63 (75, 87) sts.

Work even until armhole measures approx 6¼ (6½, 7) inches, ending Row 1 or 7 of pat.

Shape shoulders

Bind off 9 (8, 9) sts at the beg of the next 2 rows, 8 (7, 9) sts at beg of the following 2 rows, and 0 (7, 9) sts at the beg of the last 2 rows, omitting yo's as necessary at edges—

29 (31, 33) back neck sts.
Bind off.

FRONT

Work as for back until piece measures approx 2½ (2¾, 2¾) inches shorter than back, ending with Row 1 or 7 of pat.

Next row (RS): Work pat across 23 (28, 33) sts and slip to waste yarn or holder, bind off center 17 (19, 21) sts, work established pat to end.

Right front neck and shoulder

Dec 1 st at neck edge on the next 6 rows, omitting yo's as necessary at edge—17 (22, 27) sts.

Work even until front measures same as back to shoulder shaping, ending with a RS row.

Bind off 9 (8, 9) sts at beg of next row, then 8 (7, 9) sts at the beg of the following WS row, then 0 (7, 9) sts at the beg of the last WS row.

Left front neck & buttonhole band shoulder

With WS facing, join yarn at neck edge of left front.

Dec 1 st at neck edge on the next 6 rows, omitting yo's as necessary at edge—17 (22, 27) sts.

Work even until front measures 1 inch short of back to shoulder shaping, ending with a WS row.

Bind off 9 (8, 9) sts at beg of next row, then 8 (7, 9) sts at beg of the following RS row, then 0 (7, 9) sts at beg of the last RS row.

SLEEVES

Note: To keep track of the pattern while inc, place markers as indicated, moving them up on each row. This marks where rep starts and ends, so the sts before and after can be worked in the correct sequence and taken into pattern where possible.

With smaller needles and A, cast on 39 (41, 43) sts.

Knit 4 rows.

Change to B and work 2 rows St st.

Bobble Row (RS): Inc 1 B, k0 (1, 2) B, *MB with A, k5; rep from *, ending MB with A, k0 (1, 2) B, inc 1 B—41 (43, 45) sts.

Cut A.
With B, purl 1 row.
With A, knit 3 rows.

Next row (WS): K1 (2, 3), pm, work Row 1 of Honeycomb pat, pm, k1 (2, 3).

Change to larger needles and inc 1 st at each edge on Pat Row 4, then [every 4 rows] 9 (9, 10) times, 61 (63, 67) sts, [every 6 rows] 2 (2, 3) times, and [every 8 rows] twice, working new sts in pat as possible—69 (71, 77) sts (not counting yo's).

Work even until piece measures 9¼ (10¼, 11½) inches.

Place marker at each end of the row, and work even for 1¼ inches.

Bind off all sts.

ASSEMBLY

Block pieces to finished measurements.
Sew right shoulder seam.

NECKBAND

With B, crochet a row of sc around the neckline (optional).

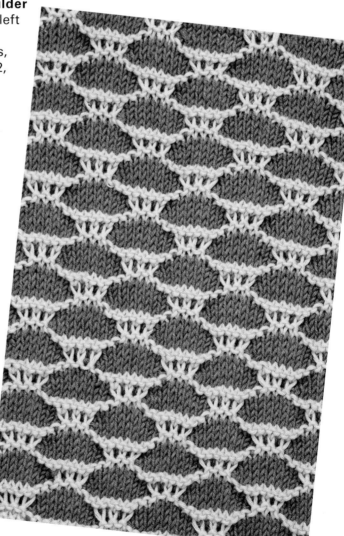

With RS facing, using smaller needles and B, pick up and knit 14 (15, 15) sts along left front neck edge, 17 (19, 21) sts across center front, 21 (22, 22) sts along right front neck edge, and 29 (31, 33) sts across back neck edge—81 (87, 91) sts.

Rows 1 (WS)–3: With B, knit.

Row 4 (RS): With A, knit and dec 4 sts evenly across—77 (83, 87) sts.

Row 5: Purl.

Bobble row: K1 A, *MB with B, k5 A; rep from * to last 4 (4, 2) sts, MB with B, k3 (3, 1) A. Cut B.

Row 7: With A, purl. Cut A.

Row 8: With B, knit.

Row 9: Knit, dec 4 sts evenly across the front—73 (79, 83) sts.

Row 10: Knit.

Bind off kwise on WS.

BUTTON BAND

With RS facing, smaller needles and B, pick up and knit 27 (31, 36) sts evenly along neckband edge and left back shoulder.

Knit 6 rows.

Bind off kwise on WS.

BUTTONHOLE BAND

With RS facing, smaller needles and B, pick up and knit 27 (31, 36) sts along left front shoulder and neckband edge.

Knit 3 rows.

Next row (RS): Working from shoulder edge, k4, *work 1 row 3-St Buttonhole over next 4 sts, k5 (7, 5); rep from * 1 (1, 2) time(s), work buttonhole over next 4 sts, k1.

Knit 2 rows.

Bind off kwise on WS.

FINISHING

Lap the buttonhole band over the button band, and sew the shoulder ends tog. Sew buttons on button band opposite buttonholes. Set in sleeves. Sew side and sleeve seams.

HAT

BODY

With smaller needle and A, cast on 96 (108) sts; pm for beg of rnd and join, taking care not to twist sts.

Work K1, P1 Rib for 1 inch.

Purl 1 rnd, knit 1 rnd, purl 1 rnd.

Change to B and knit 2 rnds.

Bobble Rnd: *K3 B, *MB with A, k2 A; rep from * around.

With B, knit 1 rnd.

With A, knit 1 rnd, purl 1 rnd, knit 1 rnd.

Change to larger needle and work 19 rnds in Honeycomb pat, ending with Rnd 7.

Next rnd: Work Rnd 1 of Stripe pat and inc 4 (2) sts evenly around—100 (110) sts.

Work Stripe pat until piece measures approx 5 ¼ (5 ½) inches, ending with Rnd 2, 4 or 6.

Next rnd: Change to smaller needle and continue established Stripe pat.

Next rnd: Continue established Stripe pat, *work 10 (11) sts, pm; rep from * around.

CROWN

Dec rnd: *Knit to 2 sts before marker, k2tog; rep from * around—90 (100) sts.

Continue in established pat, rep Dec rnd [every other rnd] 8 (9) times—10 sts.

Work 1 more rnd.

Cut yarn, leaving a 6-inch tail.

With tapestry needle, thread tail through rem sts, pull tight and secure to WS.

FINISHING

Weave in ends. Block. ∎

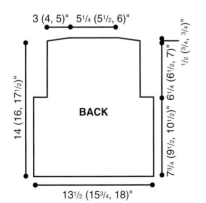

3 (4, 5)"   5¼ (5½, 6)"

½ (¾, ¾)"

6¼ (6½, 7)"

14 (16, 17½)"

7¾ (9½, 10½)"

BACK

13½ (15¾, 18)"

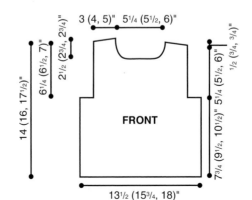

3 (4, 5)"   5¼ (5½, 6)"

2½ (2¾, 2¾)"

6¼ (6½, 7)"

½ (¾, ¾)"

5¼ (5½, 6)"

14 (16, 17½)"

7¾ (9½, 10½)"

FRONT

13½ (15¾, 18)"

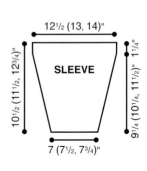

12½ (13, 14)"

1¼"

10½ (11½, 12¾)"

9¼ (10¼, 11½)"

SLEEVE

7 (7½, 7¾)"

SAUCY STRIPES PULLOVER

DESIGN BY MELISSA LEAPMAN

WHAT'S IN THE BAG

Cascade Yarns Luna (worsted weight; 100% Peruvian cotton; 82 yds/50g per hank): 4 (4, 5, 6) hanks each of teal #734 (A) and blue #721 (B)

Size 7 (4.5mm) needles or size needed to obtain gauge

SKILL LEVEL

 EASY

SIZES

Child's 2 (4, 6, 8) Instructions are given for smallest size, with larger sizes in parentheses. When only 1 number is given, it applies to all sizes.

FINISHED MEASUREMENTS

Chest: 28 (30, 32, 35) inches
Total length (with lower edge unrolled): 15 (16, 17, 18) inches

GAUGE

18 sts and 26 rows = 4 inches/10cm in St st. To save time, take time to check gauge.

SPECIAL ABBREVIATION

Make 1 (M1): Insert LH needle from front to back under the running thread between the last st worked and next st on RH needle; knit into the back of resulting loop.

PATTERN STITCH

Stripe Pattern
Work 6 rows of A in St st.
  Work 6 rows of B in St st.
  Rep these 12 rows for pat.

PATTERN NOTE

When measuring length, unroll lower edges of knitted fabric.

BACK

With A, cast on 64 (68, 72, 78) sts.
  Work even in Stripe pat until piece measures approx 8½ (9, 9½, 10) inches, ending with a WS row.

Shape armholes

Bind off 4 (5, 6, 7) sts at beg of next 2 rows—56 (58, 60, 64) sts.
  Work even until armhole measures approx 5½ (6, 6½, 7) inches, ending with a WS row.

Shape shoulders

Bind off 5 (5, 5, 6) sts at beg of next 4 rows, then 4 (5, 6, 6) sts at beg of next 2 rows—28 sts.
  Bind off.

FRONT

Work same as for back until armholes measure approx 4½ (5, 5½, 6) inches, ending with a WS row.

Shape neck & shoulders

Next Row (RS): K22 (23, 24, 26) sts; join 2nd ball of yarn

and bind off center 12 sts, knit to end of row.

Working both sides at once with separate balls of yarn, bind off at each neck edge 4 sts once then 2 sts once—16 (17, 18, 20) sts each side.

Dec 1 st at each neck edge [every row] twice; *at the same time*, when piece measures same as back to shoulders, shape shoulders same as for back.

SLEEVES
With A, cast on 30 (32, 32, 34) sts.

Work 6 rows in Stripe pat.

Inc row (RS): Continuing in Stripe pat, k1, M1, knit to last st, M1, k1—32 (34, 34, 36) sts.

Rep Inc row [every 6th row] 1 (3, 9, 14) time(s), then [every 8th row] 8 (7, 3, 0) times—50 (54, 58, 64) sts.

Work even until piece measures approx 12¾ (13½, 14½, 15½) inches.

Bind off.

FINISHING
Block pieces to finished measurements. Sew right shoulder seam.

NECKBAND
With RS facing and A, pick up and knit 70 sts along neckline.

Work even in St st until for 1½ inches.

Bind off loosely, allowing neckband to roll to RS.

ASSEMBLY
Set in sleeves.

Sew left shoulder seam, including side of neckband.

Sew sleeve and side seams. ■

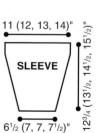

Tip While on a hike, carry along an "easy access" knapsack. Place your yarns in various plastic or drawstring bags. Zip up your bag, leaving a small opening, to "knit while you hike." You won't miss a beat enjoying the fall foliage!

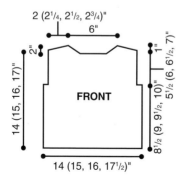

FRONT

2 (2¼, 2½, 2¾)"
6"
14 (15, 16, 17)"
2"
1"
5½ (6, 6½, 7)"
8½ (9, 9½, 10)"
14 (15, 16, 17½)"

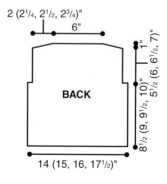

BACK

2 (2¼, 2½, 2¾)"
6"
1"
5½ (6, 6½, 7)"
8½ (9, 9½, 10)"
14 (15, 16, 17½)"

SLEEVE

11 (12, 13, 14)"
12¾ (13½, 14½, 15½)"
6½ (7, 7, 7½)"

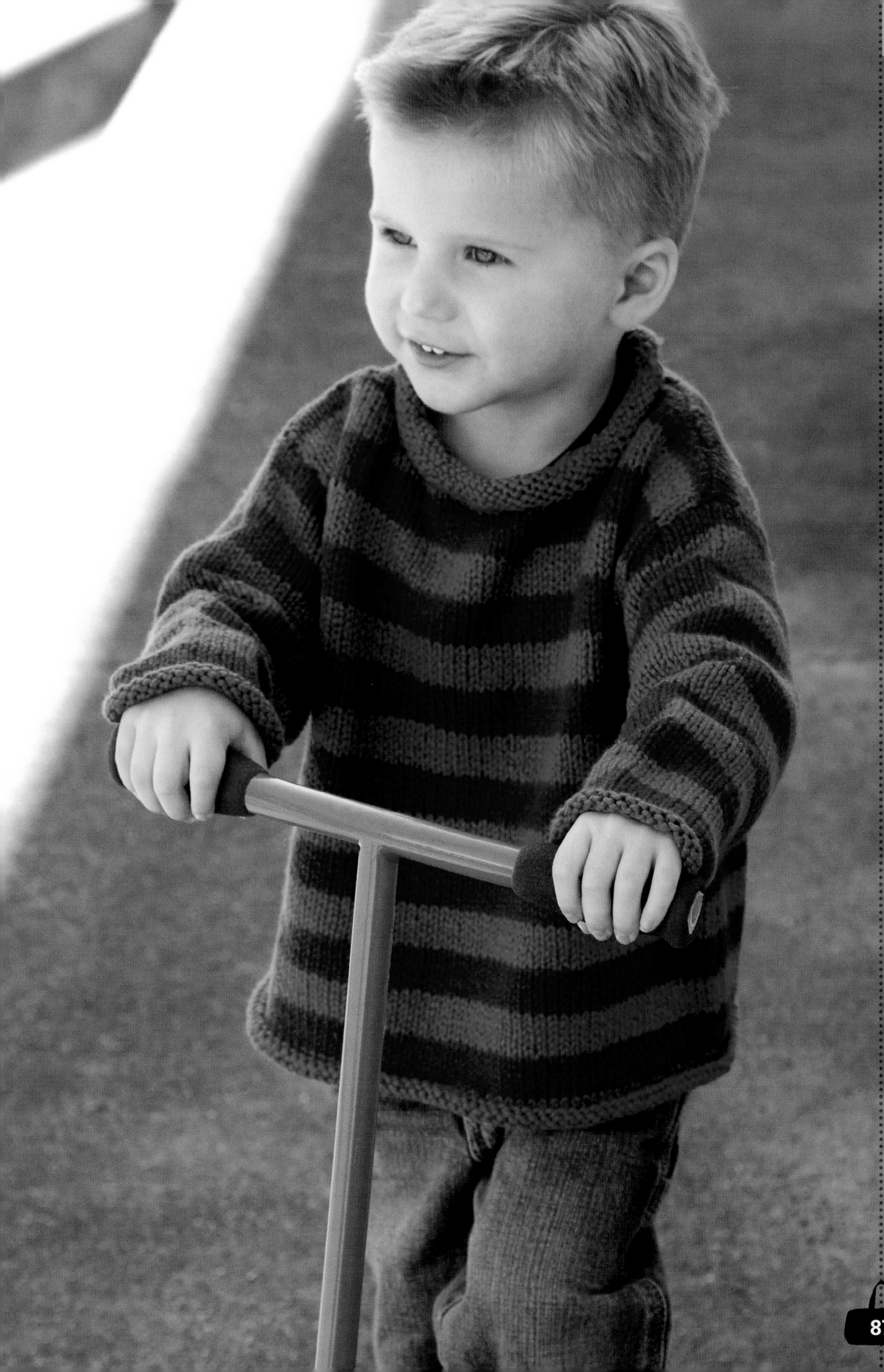

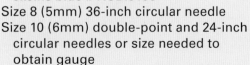

COZY HOODED SLEEPING SACK

DESIGN BY FAINA GOBERSTEIN

WHAT'S IN THE BAG

Nashua Snowbird (worsted weight; 70% wool/30% alpaca; 73 yds/50g per skein): 10 (12, 15) skeins blue # NSB.9155

4 MEDIUM

Size 8 (5mm) 36-inch circular needle
Size 10 (6mm) double-point and 24-inch circular needles or size needed to obtain gauge
Size I/9 (5.5mm) or J/10 (6mm) crochet hook
Stitch marker
Stitch holders
Six [¾-inch] buttons

SKILL LEVEL

■■■□ INTERMEDIATE

SIZES

Infant's 0–6 (6–12, 12–18) months Instructions are given for smallest size, with larger sizes in parentheses. When only 1 number is given, it applies to all sizes.

FINISHED MEASUREMENTS

Chest: 24 (32, 40) inches (buttoned)
Length: 26 (28, 30) inches
Sleeve length: 7 (7½, 8) inches

GAUGE

14 sts and 22 rnds/rows = 4 inches/10cm in Seed St Rib with larger needle.
To save time, take time to check gauge.

SPECIAL ABBREVIATIONS

M1L (Make 1 Left): Insert LH needle from front to back under the running thread between the last st worked and next st on LH needle; knit into the back of resulting loop.
M1R (Make 1 Right): Insert LH needle from back to front under the running thread between the last st worked and next st on LH needle. With RH needle, knit into the front of resulting loop.

PATTERN STITCHES

Seed Stitch (odd number of sts)
Rnd/Row 1: K1, *p1, k1; rep from * around/across.
Rnd/Row 2: Knit the purl sts and purl the knit sts as they present themselves.
    Rep Rnd/Row 2 for pat.

Seed Stitch Rib (multiple of 14 sts)
Rnd/Row 1: *Work 7 sts in Seed St, 7 sts in St st; rep from * around.
    Rep Rnd/Row 1 for pat.

SPECIAL TECHNIQUES

Provisional Cast-On: With crochet hook and waste yarn, make a chain several sts longer than desired cast on. With knitting needle and project yarn, pick up indicated number of sts in the "bumps" on back of chain. When indicated in pattern, "unzip" the crochet chain to free live sts.

3-Needle Bind-Off: With RS tog and needles parallel, using a 3rd needle, knit tog 1 st from the front needle with 1 from the back. *Knit tog 1 st each from front and back needles, and sl the first st over the 2nd to bind off; rep from * across, then fasten off last st.

PATTERN NOTE

The sack is worked in the round from bottom up, then split at center front for opening and worked back and forth in rows. The sleeves are knit in the round. The hood extends the central panel on the back.

BODY

With larger circular needle, using provisional method, cast on 83 (111, 139) sts; place marker for beg of rnd and join, taking care not to twist sts.

    Work 10 rnds Seed St.
Next rnd: Change to Seed St Rib and work to last st, k1 in front and back of last st—84 (112, 140) sts.

    Work even in Seed St Rib until piece measures 9 (10, 11) inches.

"I often travel to different countries and never miss an opportunity to visit a yarn shop. I spent one summer in Melbourne, Australia and, while visiting, I found the most amazing little shop. Since it was hard to decide what to buy, the only choice was to purchase as much yarn as I could carry. Upon my arrival in the United States, the customs officials were quite amused, noticing that I had 'smuggled' in two large suitcases of yarn!"

Divide for Front Opening

Next row (RS): Work 46 (60, 74) sts in established pat, turn.
Next row (WS): Bind off 1 st, work to last st, k1-tbl—83 (111, 139) sts.
Next row: Sl 1, work to last st, k1-tbl.

Continue working established pat back and forth, slipping first st and knitting last st tbl on all rows, until piece measures 20 (22, 23) inches, ending with WS row.

Separate for armholes

Row 1 (RS): Sl 1, work 61 (82, 103) sts in established pat, turn; put rem 21 (28, 35) sts on hold for left front.
Row 2: Sl 1, work 39 (53, 67) sts in pat, k1-tbl, turn; put rem 21 (28, 35) sts on hold for right front.

BACK

Work 41 (55, 69) back sts even in established pat, slipping first st and knitting last st tbl on all rows, until armholes measure 6 (6, 7) inches.

Place 11 (14, 18) left shoulder sts, 19 (27, 33) neck sts, 11 (14, 18) right shoulder sts on separate holders.

LEFT FRONT

Slip 21 (28, 35) left front sts from holder to larger needle and with RS facing, join yarn.

Work even in established pat, slipping first st and knitting last st tbl on all rows, until armholes measure 4 (4, 5) inches, ending with RS row.

Shape Neck

Bind off 3 sts at neck edge 3 (4, 5) times, then bind off 1 (2, 2) st(s)—11 (14, 18) sts.

Place sts on holder.

RIGHT FRONT

Slip 21 (28, 35) right front sts from holder to larger needle and with RS facing, join yarn.

Work even in established pat, slipping first st and knitting last st tbl on all rows, until armholes measure 4 (4, 5) inches, ending with WS row.

Shape Neck

Bind off 3 sts at neck edge 3 (4, 5) times, then bind off 1 (2, 2) st(s)—11 (14, 18) sts.

Place sts on holder.

SLEEVE

With dpns, cast on 33 (33, 37) sts; place marker for beg of rnd and join, taking care not to twist sts.

Work 10 rnds in Seed St.
Set-up rnd: K13 (13, 15), pm, work 7 sts Seed St, pm, k13 (13, 15).
Inc rnd: K1, M1L, knit to marker, work 7 sts in Seed St, knit to last st, M1R, k1—35 (35, 39) sts.

Continue in established pat and rep Inc rnd [every 5 rnds] 4 (4, 5) times—43 (43, 49) sts.

Work even until piece measures 7 (7½, 8) inches.

Bind off all sts.

ASSEMBLY

Weave in all ends. Block all pieces.

Join left and right shoulders using 3-Needle Bind-Off.

Unzip Provisional Cast-On, putting first 24 (31, 38) back sts on smaller circular needle, then next 42 (56, 70) front sts larger circular needle, and last 17 (24, 31) back sts on smaller circular needle. With larger dpn, join bottom using 3-Needle Bind-Off and on last st, work 2 front sts tog as you bind off.

Sew sleeves into armholes.

HOOD

With RS facing, join yarn at right front edge. With smaller circular needle, pick up and knit 18 (20, 22) sts along right neck; slip back neck sts from holder to dpn and work 19 (27, 33) sts

Rep Rows 1 and 2 until all side sts are worked in.

Leave rem 23 (23, 27) sts on needle.

BUTTON/BUTTONHOLE BAND

With RS facing and using smaller circular needle, beg at right front of opening, pick up and knit 66 (66, 66) sts along right side of opening, 25 (25, 27) sts along right side of hood, knit 23 (23, 27) top hood sts, pick up and knit 25 (25, 27) sts along left side of hood, 66 (66, 66) sts along left side of opening—205 (205, 213) sts.

Row 1 (RS): Sl 1, *p1, k1; rep from * to last st, k1-tbl.

Row 2: Sl 1, *k1, p1; rep from * to last st, k1-tbl.

Buttonhole row: Sl 1, p1, k1, *yo, k2tog, work 10 sts in established rib; rep from * 4 times, yo, k2tog, work established rib to last st, k1-tbl.

Row 4: Rep Row 2.

Row 5: Rep Row 1.

Bind off all sts in pat.

FINISHING

Position buttonhole band on top of button band and sew them together with the bottom front.

Weave in all ends and block again.

Sew on buttons opposite buttonholes. ■

in established pat; pick up and knit 18 (20, 22) sts along left neck—55 (67, 77) sts.

Rows 1 and 3 (WS): Sl 1, *k1, p1; rep from * to last 2 sts, k1, k1-tbl.

Row 2: Sl 1, *p1, k1; rep from * to last 2 sts, p1, k1-tbl.

Change to larger circular needle.

Set-up row (RS): Sl 1, k23 (29, 34), place marker, work 7 sts in Seed St, place marker, k23 (29, 34), k1-tbl.

Work even in established pat, working side sts in St st, center 5 sts in Seed St, and slipping first st and knitting last st tbl, until hood measures 7 (8, 8) inches from neckline, ending with a WS row.

Turning the hood

Row 1 (RS): Sl 1, work in pat to 7 (7, 9) sts beyond Seed St center, ssk, turn.

Row 2: Sl 1, work in pat to 7 (7, 9) sts beyond Seed St center, p2tog, turn—21 (21, 25) sts.

SLEEVE

12¼ (12¼, 14)"

7 (7½, 8)"

9½ (9½, 10½)"

HOOD

3 (4, 5)"   6¼ (7¾, 10)"

7 (8, 8)"

BODY

26 (28, 30)"

2"

6 (6, 7)"

20 (22, 23)"

24 (32, 40)"

HAPPY BABY BLANKIE

DESIGN BY KATHARINE HUNT

WHAT'S IN THE BAG

Patons Astra (DK weight; 100% acrylic; 133 yds/50g per ball): 4 balls Happy Days variegated #88713 (A)

Patons Astra (DK weight; 100% acrylic; 161 yds/50g per ball): 3 balls hot blue #08742 (B), 2 balls school bus yellow #02941 (C)

Size 6 (4mm) needles or size needed to obtain gauge

SKILL LEVEL

■■■☐ INTERMEDIATE

FINISHED SIZE

Approx 25½ x 33 inches (not including border)

GAUGE

24 sts and 35 rows= 4 inches/10cm in pat st. To save time, take time to check gauge.

PATTERN STITCHES

Slip Stitch (multiple of 8 sts + 1)
Row 1 (RS): With A, knit.
Row 2: With A, k1, *p1 wrapping yarn twice, k5, p1 wrapping yarn twice, k1; rep from * to end.
Row 3: With B (C), k1, *sl 1 (dropping extra wrap), k5, sl 1 (dropping extra wrap), k1; rep from * to end.
Rows 4 and 6: With B (C), p1, *sl 1, p5, sl 1, p1; rep from * to end.
Row 5: With B (C), k1, *sl 1, k5, sl 1, k1; rep from * to end.
Row 7: With A, k1, *drop slipped st off needle to front of work, k2, pick up dropped st and knit it; k1, sl 2, drop next slipped st off needle to front of work, pass the 2 sts just slipped back to LH needle, pick up dropped st and knit it; k2, sl 1; rep from * across, ending last rep with k1 instead of sl 1.
Row 8: With A, k3, *p1, k1, p1, k2, sl 1,

k2; rep from * to last 6 sts, p1, k1, p1, k3.
Row 9: With A, knit.
Row 10: With A, k3, *p1, wrapping yarn twice, k1, p1 wrapping yarn twice, k5; rep from * to last 3 sts, k3.
Row 11: With B (C), k3, *sl 1 (dropping extra wrap), k1, sl 1 (dropping extra wrap), k5; rep from * to last 6 sts, sl 1 (dropping extra wrap), k1, sl 1 (dropping extra wrap), k3.
Rows 12 and 14: With B (C), p3, *sl 1, p1, sl 1, p5; rep from * to last 6 sts, sl 1, p1, sl 1, p3.
Row 13: With B (C), k3, *sl 1, k1, sl 1, k5; rep from * to last 6 sts, sl 1, k1, sl 1, k3.
Row 15: With A, k1, *sl 2, drop next slipped st

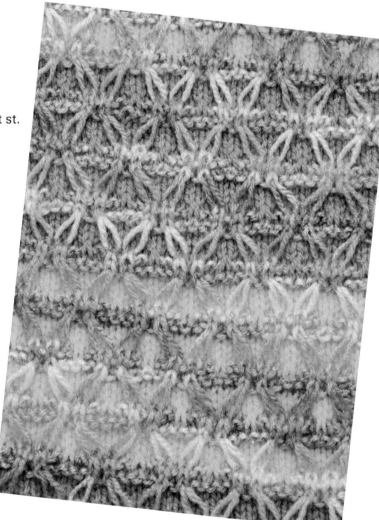

"Knitters are the only people who consider waiting in line an opportunity."

off needle to front of work, pass the 2 sts just slipped back to LH needle, pick up dropped st and knit it; k2, sl 1, drop next slipped st off needle, k2, pick up dropped st and knit it, k1; rep from * to end.

Row 16: With A, k1, *p1, k2, sl1 wyif, k2, p1, k1; rep from * to end.

Rep Rows 1–16 for pat.

Saw Tooth Edging
Row 1 (RS): K2, yo, k2tog, yo, k3—8 sts.
Row 2 and all WS rows to Row 10: Knit.
Row 3: K2, yo, k2tog, yo, k4—9 sts.
Row 5: K2, yo, k2tog, yo, k5—10 sts.
Row 7: K2, yo, k2tog, yo, k6—11 sts.

Row 9: K2, yo, k2tog, yo, k7—12 sts.
Row 11: K2, yo, k2tog, yo, k8—13 sts.
Row 12: Bind off 6 sts, k6—7 sts.

Rep Rows 1–12 rows to desired length, ending with Row 11.
Final Bind-off row: Bind off 6 sts, k1, turn, k2, turn, bind off rem sts.

PATTERN NOTE
Only 1 yarn is used per row; the color pattern is created by slipping stitches up several rows. The stripes are formed by alternating B and C in series of pattern repeats.

BLANKET
With A, cast on 145 sts.
Knit 2 rows.
*With A and B, work 2 [16-row] reps of Slip St pat.
With A and C, work 2 [16-row] reps of Slip St pat.
Rep from * 3 times.
With A and B, work 2 [16-row] reps of Slip St pat.
With A, knit 3 rows.
Bind off kwise on WS.

FINISHING
Weave in ends.
Block to finished measurements.

EDGING
With B, cast on 7 sts.
Work Saw Tooth border until it is long enough to go around perimeter of blanket; leave sts on needle.
With RS facing, using B, and beg on lower left side approx 1½ inches (or the length of 1 saw tooth), sew border around the edges of blanket. Adjust the border length, if necessary, to make it fit at the end. Sew border ends tog. ■

A-DORABLE A-LINE RUFFLED JUMPER

DESIGN BY LAURA NELKIN

WHAT'S IN THE BAG

Schaefer Yarn Lola (worsted weight; 100% merino superwash wool; 280 yds/4 oz per skein): 1 (1, 2, 2) skeins Sophia Smith

Size 7 (4.5mm) 16-inch and 24-inch circular needles or size needed to obtain gauge

Size 6 (4mm) 16-inch circular needle or 1 size smaller than that needed to obtain gauge

Stitch holders, 1 long, 2 short

Stitch markers, 1 in CC for beg of rnd

SKILL LEVEL
 EASY

SIZES
Infant's 6–12 months (12–18 months, 2T, 3T) Instructions are given for smallest size, with larger sizes in parentheses. When only 1 number is given, it applies to all sizes.

FINISHED MEASUREMENTS
Chest: 17¾ (20½, 22¼, 24) inches
Length from shoulder: 14½ (17, 20, 22½) inches

GAUGE
18 sts and 28 rnds = 4 inches/10cm in pat st with larger needle.
To save time, take time to check gauge.

PATTERN STITCHES
Slip Stitch (worked in rnds on multiple of 4 sts)
Rnd 1: *K3, sl 1; rep from * around.
Rnd 2: Knit
Rep Rnds 1 and 2 for pat.

Slip Stitch (worked in rows on multiple of 4 sts)
Row 1: *K3, sl 1; rep from * across.
Row 2: Purl.
Rep Rows 1 and 2 for pat.

PATTERN NOTE
Change to 16-inch circular needle when stitches no longer fit comfortably on 24-inch circular needle.

DRESS
Ruffle
Cast on 232 (248, 264, 280) sts; place marker for beg of rnd and join, taking care not to twist sts.
Rnd 1: *Ssk, [yo] twice, k2tog; rep from * around.
Rnd 2: *K1, [k1, p1] in double-yo, k1; rep from * around.
    Rep [Rnds 1 and 2] 3 times.
Next rnd: *[K2tog] 28 (30, 32, 34) times, k2; rep from * around—120 (128, 136, 144) sts.

Next rnd: K60 (64, 68, 72), place marker for side seam, knit to end of rnd.

Body
Work 5 (7, 9, 9) rnds in Slip St pat.
Dec rnd: *K1, ssk, knit to 3 sts before marker, k2tog, k1, slip marker; rep from * once—116 (124, 132, 140) sts.

Continue working established Slip St pat and rep Dec rnd [every 10th rnd] 0 (0, 1, 8) time(s), [every 8th rnd] 0 (3, 6, 0) time(s), [every 6th rnd] 3 (5, 1, 0) time(s) and [every 4th rnd] 6 (0, 0, 0) time(s)—80 (92, 100, 108) sts.

Work even in established Slip St pat until piece measures 9¾ (11½, 13½, 15½) inches from bottom edge, ending with Rnd 1.

Divide for armholes
Next rnd: Removing markers, k36 (42, 46, 50), bind off 7 sts, [1 st rem on RH needle], k32 (38, 42, 46) and slip to holder for front, bind off 7 sts.

BACK
Row 1 (RS): Work in pat to end of row, turn—33 (39, 43, 47) sts.
Row 2: Purl.
Dec Row: K1, ssk, work in pat to last 3 sts, k2tog, k1—31 (37, 41, 45) sts.

Continue in established pat working Dec row [every 4th row] 2 (3, 3, 3) more times—27 (31, 35, 39) sts.

Work even until armholes measure 3¾ (4½, 5½, 6) inches, ending with a WS row.

Shape back neck
Row 1 (RS): Work 5 (6, 7, 8) sts, place center 17 (19, 21, 23) sts on a holder, attach 2nd ball of yarn and work in pat to end.
Row 2: Working both shoulders at once with separate balls of yarn, purl across.
Row 3: Work to 3 sts before neck, k2tog, k1; k1, ssk, work to end—4 (5, 6, 7) sts each shoulder.

Work in pat until armholes measure 4¾ (5½, 6½, 7) inches, then slip shoulder sts to holders.

FRONT
Slip sts from holder to needle and work as for back until armholes measure 1¼ (2, 3, 4) inches, ending with a WS row.

Here's a great idea for needle storage: place one of each size circular needle into a zippered CD case. You'll never be without the size you need again!

Shape front neck
Row 1 (RS): Work 7 (8, 10, 11) sts, place center 13 (15, 15, 17) sts on a holder, attach 2nd ball of yarn and work to end.
Row 2: Working both shoulders at once with separate balls of yarn, purl across.
Row 3: Work to 3 sts before neck, k2tog, k1; k1, ssk, work to end—6 (7, 9, 10) sts each shoulder.

Rep [Rows 2 and 3] 2 (2, 3, 3) times—4 (5, 6, 7) sts each shoulder.

Work in St st until armholes measure same as for back.

FINISHING
Graft front and back shoulders tog using Kitchener st. Sew side seams.

EDGINGS
With smaller needle, pick up and knit approx 52 (62, 76, 86) sts around armhole; purl 1 rnd then bind off. Rep on 2nd armhole.

With smaller needle, pick up and knit approx 62 (66, 70, 74) sts around neckline (including sts from holders); purl 1 rnd, then bind off.

Weave in all ends.

Block to finished measurements. ■

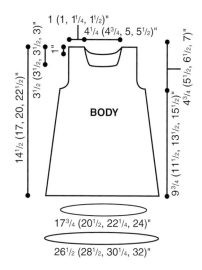

1 (1, 1¼, 1½)"

4¼ (4¾, 5, 5½)"

3½ (3½, 3½, 3)"

1"

14½ (17, 20, 22½)"

4¾ (5½, 6½, 7)"

9¾ (11½, 13½, 15½)"

BODY

17¾ (20½, 22¼, 24)"

26½ (28½, 30¼, 32)"

LITTLE SAILOR CAMI AND SOAKER PANTS

DESIGNS BY LAURA ANDERSSON

WHAT'S IN THE BAG

Crystal Palace Yarns Merino 5
  (worsted weight; 100%
  superwash wool; 110 yds/50g
  per ball): 2 (3, 3) balls each flag
  blue #5230 (A) and baby blues #2302 (B)
Size 5 (3.75mm) 16-inch circular needle
Size 8 (5mm) double-point (set of 4) and
  16-inch circular needles or size needed
  to obtain gauge
Stitch marker
Stitch holders or waste yarn

4 MEDIUM

SKILL LEVEL

 EASY

SIZES

Infant's 0–6 (6–12, 12–18) months Instructions
are given for smallest size, with larger sizes in
parentheses. When only 1 number is given, it
applies to all sizes.

FINISHED MEASUREMENTS

Shirt Circumference: 18¼ (21¼, 24½) inches
Shirt Length: 9¾ (10½, 12) inches
Soakers Circumference (waist): 18 (20½,
23½) inches

GAUGE

21 sts and 29 rnds = 4 inches/10cm in St st
using larger needle.
To save time, take time to check gauge.

PATTERN STITCH

Textured Pat (multiple of 4 sts)
Rnd 1: [P2, k2] around.
Rnd 2: [K2, p2] around.
  Rep Rnds 1 and 2 for pat.

SPECIAL TECHNIQUES

Knitted Cast-On: Make a slip knot and put on
needle. K1 into slip knot and put resulting st on LH
needle; *k1 into new st and put resulting new st
on LH needle; rep from * until all sts are cast on.
3-Needle Bind-Off: With WS tog and needles
parallel, using a 3rd needle, *knit tog the first st
on front needle and the first st on back needle;
rep from * to end. Turn and bind off pwise.

PATTERN NOTES

Shirt is worked in the round, then split for
armholes.
  Soakers are worked in the round from the
top down, then split for leg shaping.
  When working color pattern, do not carry
yarn not in use more than 3 stitches; if
necessary, catch stranded yarn with working
yarn to anchor floats.
  Watch tension when working color pattern;
if necessary, go up 1 needle size to maintain
correct gauge.

SHIRT

BODY

With larger circular needle and A, and using
knitted method, cast on 96 (112,128) sts; place
marker and join, taking care not to twist sts.

"What I like to do is make travel knitting 'kits.' I find a nice soft, see-through container. I put my entire project inside—the pattern, needles, a spare larger or smaller set of needles, scissors and yarn including an extra ball, just 'in case.'"

Purl 1 rnd.
Work 4 rnds in K2, P2 Rib; cut A.
With B, work 7 rnds in K2, P2 Rib.
Work 2 (4, 4) rnds in Textured pat.
Work 6 (10, 16) rnds in St st.
Work 4 rnds Textured pat.
Work 22 rnds following Chart, then cut A.
With B, work 2 (4, 6) rnds in Textured pat.
Knit 1 rnd, ending 5 (6, 7) sts short of marker.

DIVIDE FOR FRONT & BACK
Row 1 (RS): Bind off 10 (12, 14) sts, k38 (44, 50) and put on holder for back, bind off 10 (12, 14) sts, knit to end—38 (44, 50) sts.

Front armhole shaping
Purl 1 row.
Dec row (RS): K1, ssk, knit to last 3 sts, k2tog, k1—36 (42, 48) sts.
Continue in St st rep Dec row [every RS row] twice more, ending with a WS row—32 (38, 44) sts.

Front neck
Next row (RS): K8 (11, 14) sts, join a 2nd ball of B and bind off center 16 sts, knit to end.
Working both sides at once, continue in St st

dec 1 st at each neck edge [every row] 2 (3, 4) times—6 (8, 10) sts each shoulder.
Work even until armholes measure 3 inches, then place shoulder sts on holders; cut yarn.

BACK
With WS facing, slip back sts to needle and join A.
Work armhole shaping same as for front.
Work even until armholes measure 2 inches.

Back neck
Next row (RS): K6 (8, 10) sts, join a 2nd ball of B and bind off center 20 (22, 24) sts, knit to end.
Working even until armholes measure same as for front; leave sts on needle.

FINISHING
With B, join shoulder seams using 3-Needle Bind-Off.

Armhole edging
With larger dpns and B, beg at underarm, pick up and knit 44 sts evenly around armhole.
Work 2 rnds in K2, P2 Rib. Cut B.
With A, work 1 rnd K2, P2 Rib.
Bind off pwise.

Neck edging

With larger dpns and A, beg at left shoulder, pick up and knit 70 (76, 80) sts evenly around neck.
Bind off pwise.

FINISHING

Weave in all ends.
Block to finished measurements.

BABY SHORTS/SOAKERS

BODY

With smaller needle and B, cast on 94 (108,124) sts; place marker for beg of rnd and join, taking care not to twist sts.
Work 7 rnds in K2, P2 Rib; cut B.
With A, work 7 rnds in K2, P2 Rib.
Change to larger needle and work in St st until piece measures 7¼ (7½, 7¾) inches.

DIVIDE FOR LEGS

Next rnd: Knit to 3 (4, 5) sts before marker; bind off 6 (8, 10) sts; k41 (46, 52) sts and slip to waste yarn to hold for back; bind off 6 (8, 10) sts; knit to end—41 (46, 52) sts.

Front leg shaping

Purl 1 row.
Next row (RS): K1, [ssk] 3 times, knit to last 7 sts, [k2tog] 3 times, k1—35 (40, 46) sts.
Next row: Purl.
Rep [last 2 rows] 0 (1, 2) time(s)—35 (34, 34) sts.
Next row (RS): K1, [ssk] twice, knit to last 5 sts, [k2tog] twice, k1—31 (30, 30) sts.

Next row: Purl.
Rep [last 2 rows] 4 (3, 2) times—15 (18, 22) sts.
Next row (RS): K1, ssk, knit to last 3 sts, k2tog, k1—13 (16, 20) sts.
Next row: Purl.
Rep last 2 rows 0 (1, 0) time(s)—13 (14, 20) sts.
Place rem sts on holder.

Back leg shaping

Work as for front; leave sts on needle.
Join to front crotch sts using 3-Needle Bind-Off.

FINISHING

Leg edging

With dpns and B, pick up and knit 42 (46, 50) sts around each leg opening.
Bind off loosely pwise.
Weave in all ends. Block to finished measurements. ∎

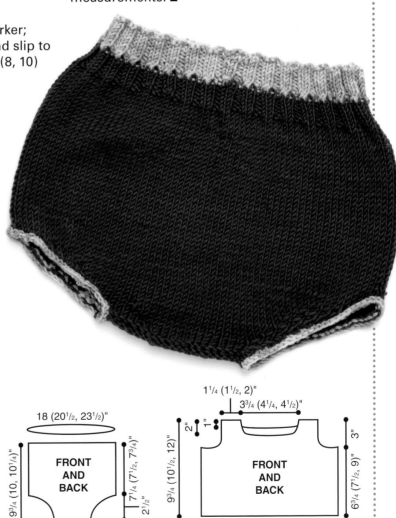

COLOR KEY
■ Knit with A
▨ Knit with B

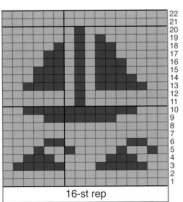

16-st rep

18 (20½, 23½)"

9¾ (10, 10¼)"

7¼ (7½, 7¾)"

2½"

FRONT AND BACK

2½ (2¾, 3¾)"

1¼ (1½, 2)"

3¾ (4¼, 4½)"

2"

1"

9¾ (10½, 12)"

3"

6¾ (7½, 9)"

FRONT AND BACK

18¼ (21¼, 24½)"

TONAL TRIANGLES KID'S PULLOVER

DESIGN BY AMY MARSHALL

WHAT'S IN THE BAG

Classic Elite Premiere (DK
  weight; 50% pima cotton/50%
  tencel; 108 yds/50g
  per hank): 3 (4, 5, 5, 6)
  hanks admiral blue #5210 (A); 2 (2, 3, 3,
  4) hanks natural #5216 (B); 2 (2, 3, 3, 3)
  hanks pastoral peri #5207 (C)
Size 6 (4mm) straight and 16-inch circular
  needles or size needed to obtain gauge
Stitch marker
Bobbins (optional)

SKILL LEVEL
■■■□ INTERMEDIATE

SIZES
Child's 2 (4, 6, 8, 10) Instructions are given for
smallest size, with larger sizes in parentheses.
When only 1 number is given, it applies to all
sizes.

FINISHED MEASUREMENTS
Chest: 21¾ (24¾, 27½, 30½, 33½) inches
Length: 14½ (16, 17½, 19, 20½) inches

GAUGE
22 sts and 26 rows = 4 inches/10cm in St st.
To save time, take time to check gauge.

PATTERN STITCH
Stripe Sequence
10 rows A
4 rows B
18 rows C
4 rows B
  Rep these 36 rows as needed.

PATTERN NOTES
The front and back of sweater are worked in
separate strips which are sewn together to
make piece, after which ribbing is added at the
bottom and neck.
  When working color charts, use intarsia

technique, using separate lengths of yarn for
each colored section; bring new color up from
under old color to lock them.
  Work chart for desired size by working
only stitches and rows within colored border
indicated for size.
  When sewing strips together with mattress
stitch, maintain a 1-stitch seam allowance.

BACK
STRIP 1
With A, cast on 17 (19, 21, 23, 25) sts.
  *With A, knit 1 row, purl 1 row.
Next row (RS): K2 A, work Chart A beg and
end where indicated for size to last 2 sts, k2 A.
  Continuing to work first and last 2 sts in St st
with A, complete chart for size being worked.
  Rep from *, working Charts B, C, D, then A
once more.
  With A, knit 1 row, purl 1 row.
  Bind off.

STRIP 2
Work as for Strip 1, but work charts in
following order: B, C, D, A, B.

STRIP 3

Work as Strip 1, but work charts in following order: C, D, A, B, C.

STRIP 4

Work as Strip 1, but work charts in following order: D, A, B, C, D.

Bottom rib

Join strips with mattress st.

With C, pick up and knit 62 (70, 78, 86, 94) sts along lower edge.

Row 1 (RS): K2, *p1, k1; rep from * to end.

Continue in established rib and work 3 rows C, 4 rows B, 4 rows A.

Bind off loosely in A.

FRONT
STRIP 1

Work as for back.

STRIP 2

Work as for back through Row 0 (2, 4, 2, 4) of last chart.

Shape right neck

Next row (RS): Bind off 11 (13, 13, 15, 15) sts, work rem 6 (6, 8, 8, 10) sts in pat.

Work 1 row even.

Dec row (RS): K1, ssk, work to end of row—5 (5, 7, 7, 9) sts.

Rep Dec row [every RS row] 4 more times—1 (1, 3, 3, 5) st(s).

Tip If you don't like to sew, weave in your loose ends with a crochet hook instead of a tapestry needle.

For Sizes 2 and 4: Bind off.

For Sizes 6, 8 and 10: Complete chart. With A, knit 1 row, purl 1 row. Bind off.

STRIP 3

Work as for back through Row 0 (2, 4, 2, 4) of last chart.

Shape left neck

Next row (RS): Work 6 (6, 8, 8, 10) sts in pat, bind off 11 (13, 13, 15, 15) sts.

Dec row (RS): Rejoin yarn; work to last 3 sts, k2tog, k1—5 (5, 7, 7, 9) sts.

Rep Dec row [every RS row] 4 more times—1 (1, 3, 3, 5) st(s).

For Sizes 2 and 4: Bind off.

For Sizes 6, 8 and 10: Complete chart. With A, work 2 rows St st. Bind off.

STRIP 4

Work as for back.

Bottom Rib

Join strips with mattress st.

Note for Sizes 2 and 4 only: Top of Strips 1 and 4 will be 6 rows longer than Strips 2 and 3.

Work bottom rib as for back.

SLEEVES

With A, cast on 32 (36, 40, 44, 44) sts.

Row 1 (RS): K2, *p1, k1, rep from * across row.

Continue in established rib and work 3 rows A, 4 rows B, 4 rows C.

Next row (RS): Change to St st, beg Stripe sequence inc 4 sts evenly across row—36 (40, 44, 48, 48) sts.

Continuing Stripe sequence in St st, work 3 rows even.

Inc row (RS): K2, M1, knit to last 2 sts, M1, k2—38 (42, 46, 50, 50) sts.

Rep Inc row [every 4 rows] 9 (11, 12, 12, 18) more times, then [every 6 rows] 4 (4, 4, 5, 3) times—64 (72, 78, 84, 92) sts.

Work even until piece measures approx 13¼ (14¼, 14¾, 16, 17½) inches.

Bind off.

FINISHING

Weave in all ends. Block all pieces to finished measurements. Join shoulder seams.

NECKBAND

With RS facing and using circular needle and C, pick up and knit 78 (86, 86, 100, 100) sts evenly around neck opening, place marker for beg of rnd.

Working in K1, P1 Rib, work 2 rnds C, 2 rnds B, 2 rnds A.

Bind off in rib.

ASSEMBLY

Sew sleeves to body. Sew side seam and underarm seams. Weave in rem ends. ■

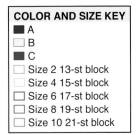

COLOR AND SIZE KEY
- ■ A
- ☐ B
- ■ C
- ☐ Size 2 13-st block
- ☐ Size 4 15-st block
- ☐ Size 6 17-st block
- ☐ Size 8 19-st block
- ☐ Size 10 21-st block

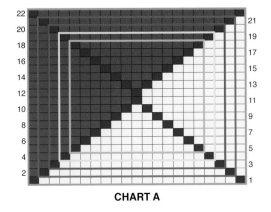

CHART A

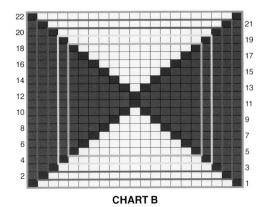

CHART B

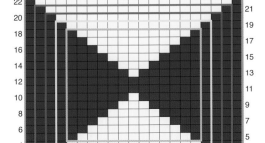

CHART C

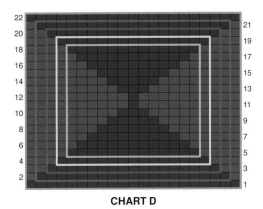

CHART D

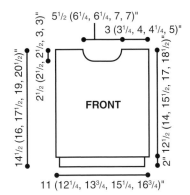

FRONT

5¹/₂ (6¹/₄, 6¹/₄, 7, 7)"

3 (3¹/₄, 4, 4¹/₄, 5)"

2¹/₂ (2¹/₂, 2¹/₂, 3, 3)"

14¹/₂ (16, 17¹/₂, 19, 20¹/₂)"

12¹/₂ (14, 15¹/₂, 17, 18¹/₂)"

2"

11 (12¹/₄, 13³/₄, 15¹/₄, 16³/₄)"

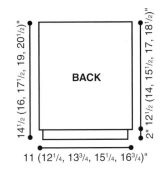

BACK

14¹/₂ (16, 17¹/₂, 19, 20¹/₂)"

12¹/₂ (14, 15¹/₂, 17, 18¹/₂)"

2"

11 (12¹/₄, 13³/₄, 15¹/₄, 16³/₄)"

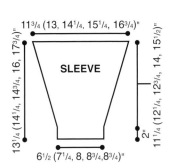

SLEEVE

11³/₄ (13, 14¹/₄, 15¹/₄, 16³/₄)"

13¹/₄ (14¹/₄, 14³/₄, 16, 17³/₄)"

11¹/₄ (12¹/₄, 12³/₄, 14, 15¹/₂)"

2"

6¹/₂ (7¹/₄, 8, 8³/₄, 8³/₄)"

GIFTY THINGS

In this chapter, you'll find an eclectic array of projects, offering a mix of fun and quirky creations, along with timeless classics. We'll keep you busy for hours on end with an inspiring collection of designs to make all of your traveling journeys memorable!

CABLE SAMPLER BABY BLOCKS

DESIGN BY DIANE ZANGL

WHAT'S IN THE BAG

Knit One Crochet Too Ty-Dy
(worsted weight; 100% cotton;
196 yds/100g per ball): 1
ball blueberry fields #631 or
pumpkin garden #541 or veranda #423

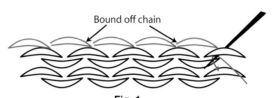

4 MEDIUM

Size 7 (4.5mm) needles
Cable needle
Stitch markers
Polyester fiberfill

SKILL LEVEL

■■■□ INTERMEDIATE

FINISHED SIZE

Approx 6-inch cube

GAUGE

Specific gauge is not critical for this project;
work at a fairly tight gauge so filling does not
show through sts.

SPECIAL ABBREVIATION

Place marker (pm): Place marker on
needle to separate pats.

BLOCKS A, B AND C

Cast on 106 sts.
Purl 1 row.
Set up pat (RS): K1, pm, work Row 1
of Chart A over next 34 sts, pm, k1,
pm, work Row 1 of Chart B over
next 34 sts, pm, k1, pm, work
Row 1 of Chart C over 34 sts,
pm, k1.
Working edge sts and
marked sts in St st and
rem sts in established
pats, work even for 31
more rows.
Bind off all sts kwise
on RS.
Cut yarn.

BLOCK D

With WS facing, pick up and purl 1 st in each of
36 center sts (Chart B sts and 2 St st side sts),
going through purl 'bump' behind each bound-
off st (see Fig. 1).

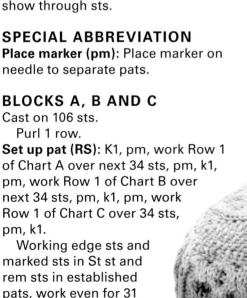

Bound off chain

Fig. 1
PICK UP PURLWISE
Insert needle under top bar of st, wrap yarn
around needle as if to purl, pull loop through stitch.

Next row (RS): K1, work Row 1 of Chart D over
next 34 sts, k1.
Working edge sts in St st and rem sts in pat
D, work even for 31 rows more.
Bind off all sts kwise on RS.
Do not cut yarn.

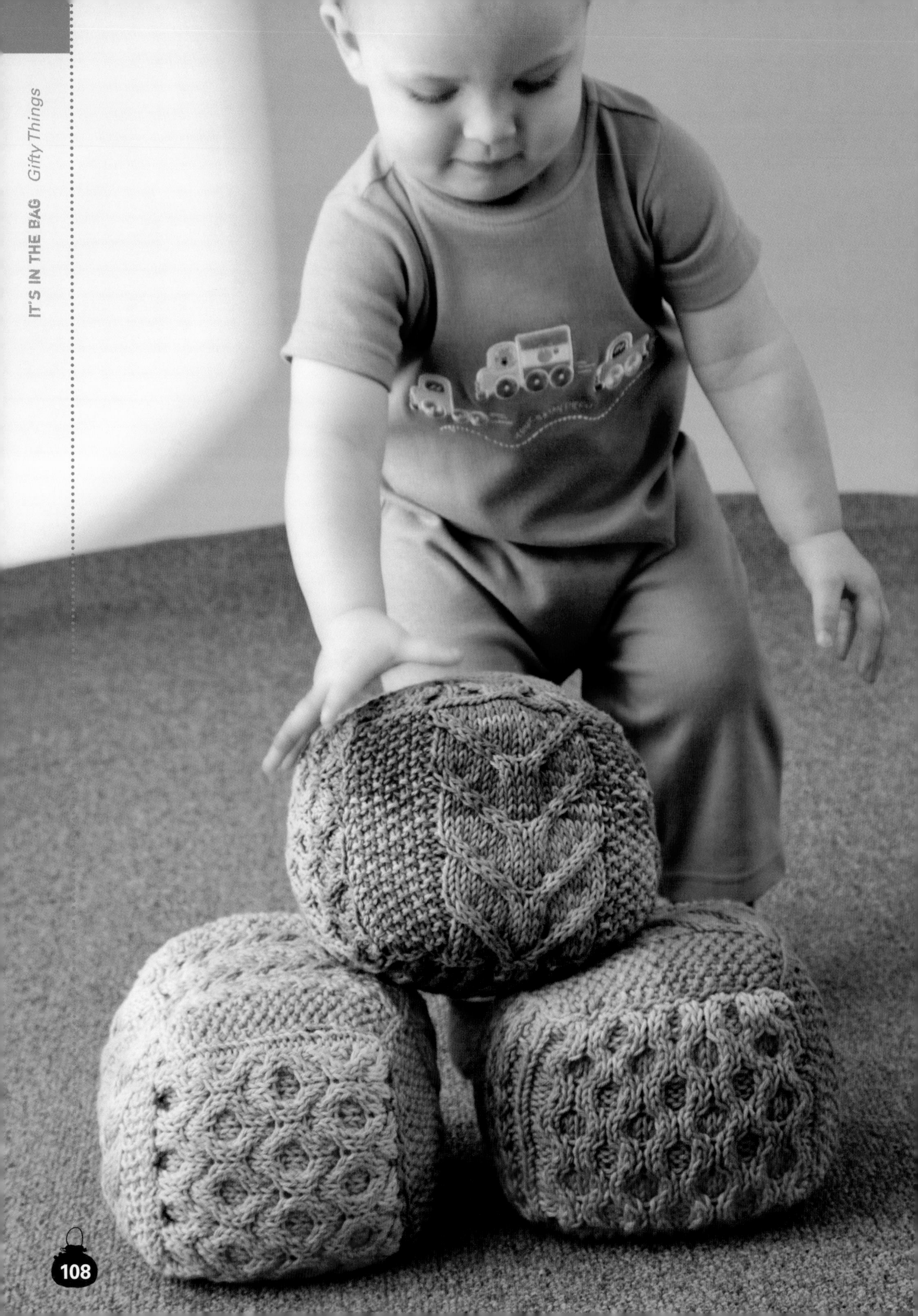

BLOCK E

With WS facing, pick up and purl 1 st in each of 36 Block D sts.

Complete as for Block D, substituting Chart E for D.

BLOCK F

With WS facing, pick up and purl 1 st in each of 36 Block E sts.

Complete as for Block D, substituting Chart F for D.

Tip If you forgot your cable needle, try a tapestry needle, a toothpick or small double-point needle.

ASSEMBLY

Weave in ends. Block piece.

Sew seams, forming a box with an open lid. Stuff with fiberfill. Sew rem seams. ∎

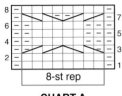

CHART A

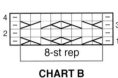

CHART B

CHART C

STITCH KEY

☐ K on RS, p on WS

– P on RS, k on WS

Sl 2 to cn and hold in front, p2, k2 from cn.

Sl 2 to cn and hold in back, k2, p2 from cn.

Sl 2 to cn and hold in front, k2, k2 from cn.

Sl 2 to cn and hold in back, k2, k2 from cn.

Sl 2 to cn and hold in front, k4, k2 from cn.

Sl 4 to cn and hold in back, k2, k4 from cn.

Sl 4 to cn and hold in front, k4, k4 from cn.

Sl 4 to cn and hold in back, k4, k4 from cn.

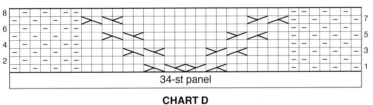

CHART D

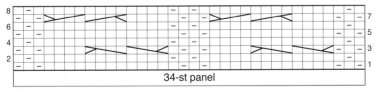

CHART E

CHART F

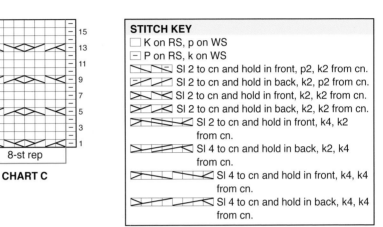

109

NAUTICAL STRIPES ONESIE & SUNHAT

DESIGNS BY KARA GOTT WARNER

WHAT'S IN THE BAG

Tahki Torino (worsted weight; 100% extra fine merino wool; 94 yds/50g per ball): 2 (2, 3) balls each light blue heather #135 (A), cream heather #134 (B) and grey heather #136 (C)

4 MEDIUM

Size 8 (5mm) straight, double-point (set of 4) and 16-inch circular needles or size needed to obtain gauge

Stitch markers, 1 in CC for beg of rnd

5 (size 3) Dritz nickel-plated brass snaps

Sewing thread to match yarn

SKILL LEVEL

■■■□ INTERMEDIATE

SIZES

Onesie: Infant's 0–3 (3–6, 6–12) months
Hat: Infant's 0–6 (6–12) months Instructions are given for smallest size, with larger sizes in parentheses. When only 1 number is given, it applies to all sizes.

FINISHED MEASUREMENTS

Chest: 20¾ (22, 24) inches
Total length to shoulder (hemmed): 11 (13, 15½) inches
Hat circumference: 14 (16) inches

GAUGE

19 sts and 26 rows/rnds = 4 inches/10cm in St st.
To save time, take time to check gauge.

SPECIAL ABBREVIATIONS

Place marker (pm): Place marker on needle to separate sections.
Make 1 Left (M1L): Insert LH needle from front to back under the running thread between the last st worked and next st on LH needle. With RH needle, knit into the back of this loop.
Make 1 Right (M1R): Insert LH needle from back to front under the running thread between the last st worked and next st on LH needle. With RH needle, knit into the front of this loop.

PATTERN STITCHES

Stripe Sequence (Onesie): *Work 14 rnds/rows St st in A, 14 rnds/rows B, 14 rnds/rows C; rep from * to end of piece.
Stripe Sequence (Hat): *Knit 8 rnds A, 8 rnds C, 8 rnds B; rep from * to end of piece.

PATTERN NOTES

Raglan-shaped onesie is worked in the round from top to armholes, then divided into body and sleeves. The body continues in the round from armholes to crotch at which point the piece is split at center front/back for legs (worked back and forth in rows). Sleeves are worked in the round.

Hat is worked from bottom to top, starting with the brim; change to double-point needles when stitches no longer fit comfortably on circular needle.

ONESIE

COLLAR

With circular needle and B, cast on 54 (56, 64) sts; pm for beg of rnd and join, taking care not to twist sts.

Work 1½ inches in St st and on last rnd, place raglan shaping markers as follows: K2 (3, 3) st, pm, k25 (25, 29), pm, k2 (3, 3), pm, k25 (25, 29).

Raglan yoke

Change to A and beg working 14-rnd/row Stripe Sequence.
Inc rnd: Slipping markers, *k1, M1L, knit to 1 st before marker, M1R, k1; rep from * around—62 (64, 72) sts.

Rep Inc rnd [every 2 (3, 3) rnds] 10 (2, 4) times, then [every 2 rnds] 0 (9, 7) times—142 (152, 160) sts.

"Some time ago, I took a ski trip to Vermont with some friends. Happily, I was not driving. Since this was a 6 hour trip, it was, of course, a perfect opportunity to knit! My chosen projects were a ski hat and mittens that I was determined to finish before my arrival. I began to knit at warp speed, but soon after we got on our way, it started to get dark. Eventually, I couldn't see a thing! Since I was working in stockinette, I relied on my fingers to see, and by the time we made it to the resort, my hat and mittens were done. And yes, I even wove in those loose ends!"

Separate sections

Next rnd: *Knit to marker, then slip 26 (28, 29) sts to waste yarn for sleeve; knit to next marker; rep from * once—90 (96, 102) body sts rem, with 45 (48, 51) sts each front and back.

BODY

Rnd 1: Cast on 4 (4, 6) sts for underarm, work front sts, cast on 4 (4, 6) sts for 2nd underarm, work back sts, place marker for beg of rnd—98 (104, 114) sts.

Work even until piece measures 5¾ (7, 8¾) inches from armhole; cut yarn.

Shape crotch and legs

Slip first 27 (28, 32) sts and last 22 (24, 25) sts to waste yarn, splitting body in half at center

front/back—49 (52, 57) sts rem on needle.
Row 1 (RS): Reattach yarn; k2, [ssk] twice, knit to last 6 sts, [k2tog] twice, k2—45 (48, 53) sts.
Row 2: Purl.

Rep [Rows 1 and 2] once more—41 (44, 49) sts.

Work even until legs measure 2 (2¼, 2½) inches from beg of crotch, ending with a WS row.

Leg Hem

Turning row (RS): Purl.

Work 3 rows in St st.
Bind off.
Rep for other side.

SLEEVES

Slip sleeve sts from waste yarn to double-point needles.
Row 1 (RS): Maintaining established Stripe Sequence, cast on 2 (2, 3) sts for underarm, knit across sleeve sts, cast on 2 (2, 3) sts for underarm, pm for beg of rnd and join—30 (32, 35) sts.

Work even in St st until sleeve measures 2 (2½, 2½) inches.

Sleeve Hem

Turning rnd: Purl.

Knit 3 rnds.
Bind off.

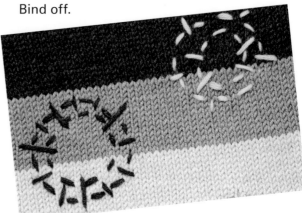

FINISHING

Sew sleeve and body sts tog at underarms.

Fold up sleeve and leg hems at turning ridge and sew to WS. With B, sew running stitch in middle of hem. With colors of choice, sew dashed circle designs randomly around hat (see Figs 1 and 2).

Fig.1
Basic Running Stitch
Thread yarn onto tapestry needle.
Starting from the WS, *draw needle up through A, then down into B; rep from *.

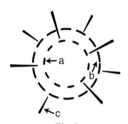

Fig.2
Dashed Circle
Work 2 concentric circles with random rays as follows:
Thread yarn onto tapestry needle.
A: Starting from WS, draw needle up through first stitch for smaller circle; work Basic Running Stitch until circle is complete.
B: Work larger circle same as for A.
C: Work single short and long stitches randomly around circles.

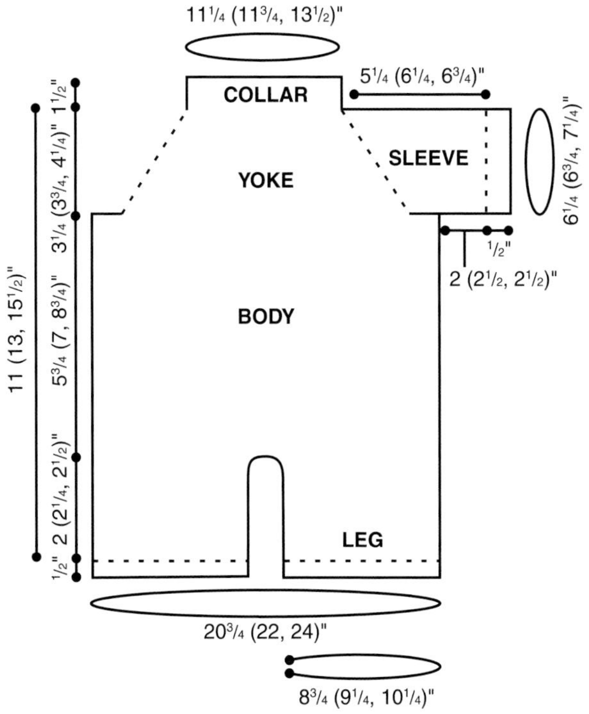

Weave in loose ends. Block to finished measurements.

Sew on 5 sets of snaps to close crotch, 1 in center crotch and 2 on each leg.

HAT

BRIM

With circular needle and A, cast on 90 (93) sts, pm every 30 (31) sts.

Knit 3 rnds.

Dec rnd: Slipping markers, *k1, k2tog, knit to 3 sts before marker, ssk, k1; rep from * around—84 (87) sts.

Purl 1 rnd for turning ridge.

Beg 8-rnd Stripe Sequence and work Dec rnd—78 (81) sts.

Knit 3 rnds.

Rep Dec rnd—72 (75) sts.

BODY AND CROWN

Maintaining Stripe Sequence, knit 14 rnds.

Rep Dec rnd on next then [every other rnd] 9 times—12 (15) sts.

Cut yarn, leaving a 6-inch tail.

Using tapestry needle, thread tail through rem sts, and pull tight.

Weave in all ends.

FINISHING

Fold up hem at turning ridge and sew to WS. With C, sew running stitch in middle of hem edge. With colors of choice, sew dashed circle designs randomly around hat (see Figs 1 and 2).

Block. ∎

Schematic measurements

11¼ (11¾, 13½)"

COLLAR

5¼ (6¼, 6¾)"

1½

3¼ (3¾, 4¼)" 1½

SLEEVE

YOKE

6¼ (6¾, 7¼)"

11 (13, 15½)"

5¾ (7, 8¾)"

½"

2 (2½, 2½)"

BODY

2 (2¼, 2½)"

LEG

½"

20¾ (22, 24)"

8¾ (9¼, 10¼)"

CUTE AS A BUTTON BABY SET

DESIGNS BY CHRISTINE L. WALTER

WHAT'S IN THE BAG

Knit One Crochet Too Babyboo
  (DK weight; 55% nylon/45%
  bamboo; 115 yds/50g per ball):
  4 (5, 5) balls lilac #719
Size 6 (4 mm) double-point (set of 5) and
  16-inch circular needles or size needed
  to obtain gauge
5 (½-inch) buttons
1 yard ribbon for booties (optional)

3 LIGHT

SKILL LEVEL

■■□□ EASY

SIZES
Jacket: Newborn (3–6 months, 6–9 months)
Hat: Small/medium (medium/large)
Booties: Small/medium (medium/large)
Instructions are given for smallest size, with
larger sizes in parentheses. When only 1
number is given, it applies to all sizes.

FINISHED MEASUREMENTS
Sweater chest: 19¼ (21¼, 24¼) inches
(buttoned)
Sweater length: 10 (11, 12) inches
Hat circumference: 14 (16) inches
Foot length: 4 (5) inches

GAUGE
17 sts and 32 rows = 4 inches/10 cm in Eyelet
Lace (after blocking).
19 sts and 27 rows = 4 inches/10 cm in St st.
To save time, take time to check gauge.

SPECIAL ABBREVIATION
Knit in Front and Back of Stitch (k1f&b): K1
in front and back of st to inc 1.

PATTERN STITCH
Eyelet Lace (multiple of 3 sts + 3)
Row 1 and all WS rows: Purl.
Row 2 (RS): K2, *k2tog, yo, k1; rep from *
to last st, k1.

Row 4: K2, *yo, k1, k2tog; rep from * to last
st, k1.
  Rep Rows 1–4 for pat.

PATTERN NOTE
When knitting hat, change to double-
point needles when stitches no longer fit
comfortably on circular needle.

JACKET

BACK
Cast on 42 (45, 51) sts.
  Knit 5 rows.
  Work in Eyelet Lace until piece measures
10 (11, 12) inches, ending with a RS row.
  Bind off pwise.

RIGHT FRONT
Cast on 18 (21, 24) sts.
  Knit 5 rows.
  Work in Eyelet Lace until piece measures
8½ (9, 10) inches, ending with a WS row.

Neck shaping
With RS facing, continue in pat and bind off
2 sts at neck edge [every RS row] 1 (2, 3)
times—16 (17, 18) sts.
  Bind off 1 st at neck edge [every RS row]
3 times—13 (14, 15) sts.
  Work even in pat until piece measures same
as back, ending with a RS row.
  Bind off pwise.

LEFT FRONT
Work as for right front to neck shaping, ending
with a RS row.

Tip Plastic, sealable containers are
a great solution for organizing
projects in your car trunk. Why
not keep an extra container on hand
with a selection of yarns for future projects.

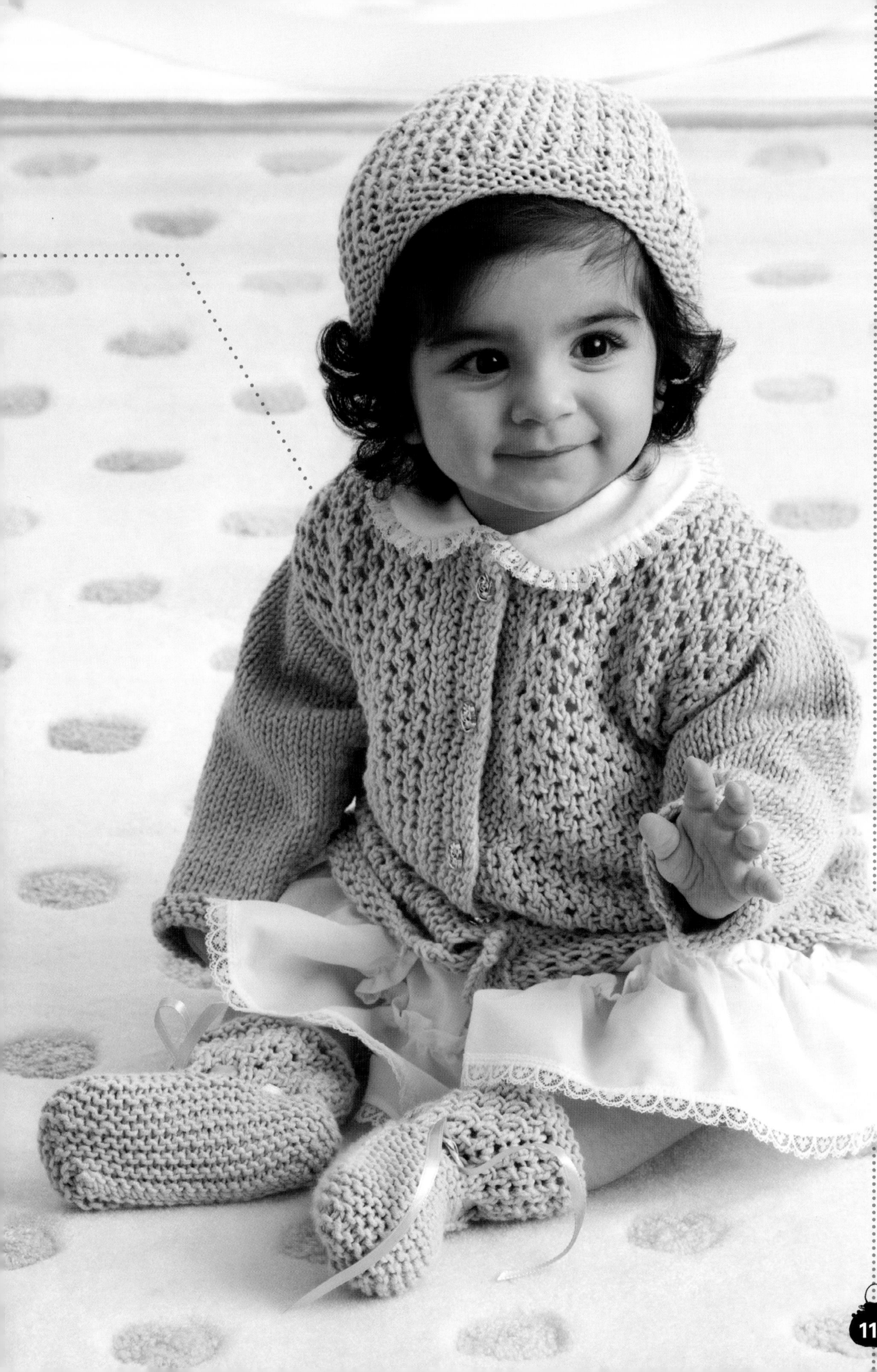

Neck shaping

With WS facing, continue in pat and bind off 2 sts at neck edge [every WS row] 1 (2, 3) times—16 (17, 18) sts.

Bind off 1 st at neck edge [every WS row] 3 times—13 (14, 15) sts.

Work even in pat until piece measures same as back, ending with a RS row.

Bind off pwise.

SLEEVES

Cast on 28 (30, 30) sts.

Knit 5 rows.

Inc row (RS): K1, k1f&b, knit to last 2 sts, k1f&b, k1—30 (32, 32 sts).

Continue in St st and rep Inc row [every 4 rows] 8 (9, 11) times—46 (50, 54) sts.

Work even until piece measures 6½ (7, 8) inches.

Bind off.

FINISHING

Weave in all ends. Block pieces. Sew shoulder seams. Mark armholes by placing markers 4¾ (5¼, 5½) inches down from shoulders on fronts and back. Sew sleeves between markers. Sew side and sleeve seams.

NECK EDGING

With RS facing, pick up and knit 47 (49, 57) sts around neck.

Knit 3 rows.

Bind off pwise on RS.

BUTTONHOLE BAND

With RS facing, pick up and knit 42 (46, 48) sts along appropriate front edge (right side for girl's sweater, left side for boy's sweater) between cast-on edge and neck edging.

Knit 3 rows.

Buttonhole row: K2 (2, 4), *yo, k2tog, k7 (8, 8); rep from * to last 4 sts, yo, k2tog, k2.

Knit 3 rows.

Bind off kwise on WS.

BUTTON BAND

With RS facing, pick up and knit 42 (46, 48) sts along opposite front edge.

Knit 8 rows.

Bind off kwise on WS.

Weave in ends.

HAT

BODY

Using dpns or short circular needle, cast on 60 (66) sts; place marker for beg of rnd and join, taking care not to twist sts.

Rnds 1, 3, 5: Purl

Rnds 2, 4, 6: Knit.

Rnd 7: *K2tog, yo, k1; rep from * around.

Rnd 8: Knit.

Rnd 9: *Yo, k1, k2tog; rep from * around.

Rep Rnds 6–9 until hat measures 4 (4½) inches.

SHAPE CROWN

Rnd 1: *K4, k2tog; rep from * around—50 (55) sts.

Rnd 2 and all even-numbered rnds: Purl.

Rnds 3 and 5: Knit.

Rnd 7: *K3, k2tog; rep from * around—40 (44) sts.

Rnd 9: Knit.

Rnd 11: *K2, k2tog; rep from * around—30 (33) sts.

Rnd 13: *K4, k2tog; rep from * to last 0 (3) sts, k0 (3)—25 (28) sts.

Rnd 15: *K3, k2tog; rep from * last 0 (3) sts, k0 (3)—20 (23) sts.

Rnd 17: *K2, k2tog; rep from * around—15 (18) sts.

Rnd 19: *K1, k2tog; rep from * around—10 (12) sts.

Rnd 21: *K2tog; rep from * around—5 (6) sts. Cut yarn leaving a 6-inch tail.

With tapestry needle, thread tail through rem sts, pull tight and secure to WS.

Weave in ends.

BOOTIES

CUFF/HEEL

Cast on 27 (33) sts.

Knit 4 rows.

Beg with Row 2, work 11 (15) rows in Eyelet Lace.

Next row (RS): K18 (22) sts, turn, leaving rem sts unworked.

Next row: K9 (11) sts, turn, leaving rem sts unworked.

Working on center 9 (11) sts, knit 12 (16) rows.

Next row (RS): K9 (11), pick up and knit 7 (9) sts along left side of flap, knit across rem 9 (11) sts, turn—25 (31) sts.

Next row: K25 (31), pick up and knit 7 (9) sts along right side of flap then knit rem 9 (11) sts—41 (51) sts.

SHAPE FOOT

Row 1 (RS): K1, k2tog, k15 (19), k2tog, k1 (3), k2tog, k15 (19), k2tog, k1—37 (47) sts.

Rows 2 and 4: Knit.

Row 3: K1, k2tog, k13 (18), k2tog, k1, k2tog, k13 (18), k2tog, k1—33 (43) sts.

Row 5: K1, k2tog, k11 (16), k2tog, k1, k2tog, k11 (16), k2tog, k1—29 (39) sts.

Bind off kwise on WS.

Cut yarn, leaving a long tail.

FINISHING

Sew seam from toe/sole to top cuff. Weave in ends.

Optional: Thread ribbon through eyelets closest to foot and tie in bow. ∎

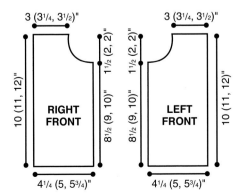

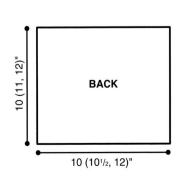

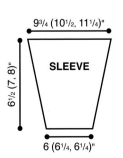

DAY AT THE BEACH FLIP-FLOPS & BRACELET

DESIGNS BY ELLEN EDWARDS DRECHSLER

WHAT'S IN THE BAG

Plymouth Fantasy Linen (worsted weight; 72% mercerized cotton/17% rayon/11% linen; 130 yds/100g per skein): 1 skein brown #5

Size 5 (3.75mm) double-point needles (flip-flops)

Size 3 (3mm) double-point needles (bracelet)

Stitch holder

Beading needle (with large eye)

Toggle set (bracelet)

Pair of thong sandals

Assorted beads (size E and larger) with large holes (the number you need may vary depending upon the size of your beads and the size of your flip-flops—sample flip-flops required approx 56 inches of strung beads; bracelet required approx 55 beads)

SKILL LEVEL

■■□□ EASY

FINISHED SIZE

As desired by knitter

GAUGE

Gauge is not critical for this project.

SPECIAL ABBREVIATION

Bring Up Bead (BUB): Slide up a bead and work next st.

PATTERN NOTES

If you want your flip-flops to match, divide the skein into 2 balls and string beads in same order onto each ball of yarn.

If you have a large bead or a long bead, work the adjacent stitches without a bead to allow more room for the bigger bead.

Beads should sit between stitches and show on the purl side of the fabric.

If you run out of pre-strung beads, you can add beads to the non-working end of the yarn.

Make the bracelet tight because the weight of the beads will cause the bracelet to stretch out over time.

FLIP-FLOPS

With beading needle, thread variety of beads onto approx 56 inches of yarn.

TOE THONG

Leaving a long tail and using larger needles, cast on 7 sts.

Row 1 (WS): Knit 1 row, weaving in yarn end as you knit.

Row 2 (RS inc row): P1, M1, purl to last st, M1, p1—9 sts.

Row 3: K3, [BUB, k1] 3 times, k3.

Rep Inc row [every RS row] 4 times, and *at the same time*, gradually inc the number of beads being used on WS rows to 7 per row, placing them in the center of the row—17 sts.

Work even until toe thong measures approx 1½ inches, ending with a WS row.

STRAP 1

Next row (RS): P9, slip rem 8 sts to holder.

Leaving the first and last 2 sts bead-free, and bringing up a bead between each of the center 5 sts on WS rows, work even in rev St st on the 9 sts until knitted beaded material is approx the

"If you really want people to stare, try knitting at the gym. I usually take a small, light-weight project. I place my yarn in a small, sporty bag, which hangs off the elliptical machine. I place the instructions on the machine's control panel, and I'm ready to workout!"

length of your sandal strap (for the model, strap measures 6 inches).

Work 4 rows without beads.

Bind off and cut yarn, leaving a very long tail for sewing.

STRAP 2

Slip sts from holder to needle.

Working as for Strap 1, inc 1 st on first row—9 sts.

Complete as for Strap 1.

FINISHING

Place the toe thong portion of the fabric (purl side out) around the sandal thong, then sew sides tog with mattress st.

Using tail, sew edges of 1 strap tog to encase the sandal strap; rep on other strap.

Weave in all ends.

BRACELET

With beading needle, thread approx 55 beads onto yarn.

Thread 1 end of jewelry toggle.

Using smaller needles, cast on 4 sts.

Knit 1 row, sliding the toggle in between the 3rd and 4th sts.

Purl 1 row, weaving in the tail as you work.

Continue in St st, sliding up beads between each st on knit rows.

Work even until piece measures slightly less than your wrist circumference.

Measure off enough yarn for 3 additional rows and a bind off row, then cut the yarn.

Thread the other end of the toggle set onto the tail.

Work 2 sts, slide up the toggle, work rem 2 sts.

Work 2 more rows without beads.

Bind off.

Weave in ends. ■

ANDREA BEADED CUFFS

DESIGNS BY LAURA NELKIN

WHAT'S IN THE BAG

Schaefer Yarn Andrea (lace weight; 100% cultivated silk; 1093 yds/3.5 oz per skein): 1 skein in Laura Ingalls Wilder and Greenjeans or 40 yds of any lace weight yarn

 **SUPER FINE**

Size 0 (2mm) needles or size needed to obtain gauge
Size 1 (2.25mm) double-point needles or 1 size larger than that needed to obtain gauge
Size 8/0 seed beads (approx 8g)
Size C/2 (2.75) crochet hook
Dental floss threader
Crochet hook
Slide clasp (optional)

SKILL LEVEL

■■■□ INTERMEDIATE

SIZES

Extra-small (small, medium, large) Instructions are given for smallest size, with larger sizes in parentheses. When only 1 number is given, it applies to all sizes.

FINISHED MEASUREMENTS

Length: 5½ (6½, 7½, 8½) inches
Width: 1¼ inches (Beaded Twist Cuff);
1¾ inches (Diamond Cuff)

GAUGE

Beaded Twist Cuff: 48 sts and 44 rows = 4 inches/10cm with smaller needles.
Diamond Cuff: 52 sts and 48 rows = 4 inches/10cm with smaller needles.
To save time, take time to check gauge.

SPECIAL TECHNIQUE

Provisional Cast-On: With crochet hook and waste yarn, make a chain several sts longer than desired cast-on. With knitting needle and project yarn, pick up indicated number of sts in the "bumps" on back of chain. When indicated in pattern, "unzip" the crochet chain to free live sts.

PATTERN NOTE

If you don't want to work I-cord loops and beaded clasps to close the cuff, purchase a sew-on clasp or decorative hook and eye to finish your cuff. If you do this, work 2nd short end with plain attached I-cord.

BEADED TWIST CUFF

Using dental floss threader, thread 54 (66, 78, 90) beads onto yarn.
   With smaller needles, cast on 12 sts.
   Knit 2 rows.
   Work Beaded Twist chart 9 (11, 13, 15) times.
   Knit 2 rows.
   Bind off.
   Thread 52 (64, 76, 88) additional beads onto yarn.
   Continue with I-cord instructions below.

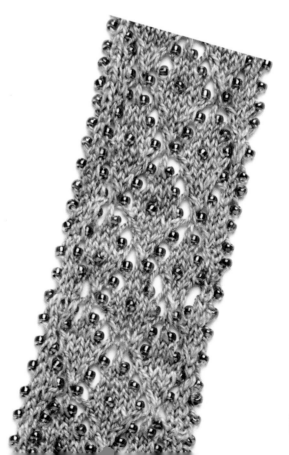

DIAMOND CUFF

Using dental floss threader, thread 135 (162, 189, 216) beads onto yarn.

With smaller needles, cast on 17 sts.

Knit 2 rows.

Work Diamond chart 5 (6, 7, 8) times.

Knit 2 rows.

Bind off.

Thread 58 (70, 82, 94) additional beads onto yarn.

Continue with I-cord instructions below.

I-CORD

Note: Instructions are given for Beaded Twist Cuff with Diamond Cuff instructions in parentheses.

With dpn and beg at top LH corner, work a 2-st attached beaded I-cord along the outside edge of the cuff as follows: Using provisional method, cast on 2 sts onto 1 dpn, and with same dpn, pick up (but do not knit) 1 st from edge of cuff—3 sts on needle.

Row 1: K1 with bead, skp, pick up 1 st from edge (but do not knit); slide sts to other end of dpn—3 sts.

Row 2: K1, skp, pick up 1 st from edge (but do not knit); slide sts to other end of dpn—3 sts.

Rep Rows 1 and 2 all the way down one long side of the cuff.

When you reach the first short side, discontinue the use of beads and continue the attached I-cord.

Resume using beads along the other long side of the cuff.

On the 2nd short side, create loops to fasten the cuff as follows: Discontinue using beads and work 2 (3) rows of attached I-cord.

*Work a 2-st unattached I-cord for 6 rows.

Skipping 1 st, pick up next st of edging and work attached I-cord for 5 (8) rows.

Rep from *, but finish by working only 2

(3) more rows of attached I-cord.

Unzip Provisional Cast-On; graft sts tog with live sts from beg of I-cord.

BEADED CLASPS
Make 2

String 3 beads onto yarn with a small sewing needle; leaving a 3-inch tail, go back through the beads again, creating a loop.

String 3 more beads and go back through the first 3 beads again; you will have a circle of 6 beads, with a length of yarn running through the middle of it (see Diagram).

Yarn running through middle of beaded circle

BEADED CLASP DIAGRAM

Sew beaded clasps to the opposite end of the bracelet in line with 2 loops, sewing only on the center thread. This is important so that the loop can go all the way around the "button" and catch itself.

FINISHING

Weave in ends and block. ∎

Tip

Here's an idea for this incredibly portable and quick project you can throw in your purse: Wind off enough yarn for each cuff, string the beads, and place the yarn along with short needles, notions, and copy of the chart cut down to size and taped onto an index card into a plastic sandwich bag.

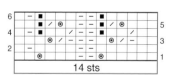

BEADED TWIST CUFF

14 sts

STITCH KEY

☐	K on RS, p on WS
–	P on RS, k on WS
○	Yo
╱	K2tog
╲	Ssk
⋏	S2KP2
✳	Slip up 1 bead and K1
⊙	Slip up 1 bead and Yo
■	No stitch

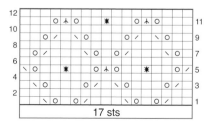

17 sts

DIAMOND CUFF

EASY AS 1-2-3 BRAIDED BELT

DESIGN BY JULIE GADDY

WHAT'S IN THE BAG

Knit One Crochet Too Wick
(worsted weight; 53% soy/47%
polypropylene; 120 yds/50g per
ball): 1 ball painted daisies #565

4 MEDIUM

Size 4 (3.5mm) double-point needles (2)
or size needed to obtain gauge
Waste yarn or 3 safety pins
2 D-rings or O-rings with at least 1³⁄₁₆ inch
inside diameter
1 yd of ⅜ inch grosgrain ribbon and
matching sewing thread (optional)

SKILL LEVEL

 INTERMEDIATE

SIZES

Woman's small/medium (medium/large)
Instructions are given for smaller size, with
larger size in parentheses. When only 1
number is given, it applies to both sizes.
Directions for custom sizing are also included
following other sizes.

FINISHED SIZE

1 x 29-33 (35-40, custom) inches

GAUGE

24 sts and 56 rows = 4 inches/10cm in Double-
Knitting.
Gauge is not critical to this project.

PATTERN STITCH

Double-Knitting (even number of sts)
Row 1: *Sl 1 wyif, k1; rep from * across.
Rep Row 1 for pat.

SPECIAL TECHNIQUE

4-St I-Cord: *K4, do not turn, slip sts back to LH
needle; rep from * until cord is desired length.

PATTERN NOTES

The gauge for the belt is significantly tighter
than the recommended gauge for the yarn.

This is to give the belt more body.

Size M/L takes the entire ball. If you are making
a custom size and plan to fit waist size larger
than 40 inches, you will need a second ball.

BELT

Flap and Tab

Cast on 6 sts.

Work 10 rows in St st, ending with a WS row.

Set-up row: *Yo, k1; rep from * across—12 sts.

Work in Double-Knitting for 5 (6) inches.

For custom size, knit until belt measures 5
inches from beg of double-knit section.

Divide for I-Cord

Divide sts into 3 groups of 4 sts and slip 2nd
and 3rd groups to a safety pin or waste yarn.

*Work 4-st I-cord for 35 (43) inches; slip sts
to safety pin or waste yarn.

Cut yarn leaving tail approx 2 yds long to use
for adjusting length of cords when braiding.

Rep from * for the rem 2 groups of 4 sts.

For custom size, knit I-cord 1½ times the
length of the completed braid.

BRAID

Lay belt on a flat surface and braid the 3 cords,
making a firm braid to minimize stretching
during wear; braid should measure 22 (27)
inches or 10 inches less than finished waist
measurement. Adjust length of cords by
adding or subtracting rows of I-cord.

TAB

Slip the 12 sts to 1 dpn.

Tip

Here's a great way to be an
"inconspicuous knitter": If you're
working on a small project, why
not try 12-inch circular needle? Simply
pull out the portion you're working on, and
then when you're done, coil it up, and place it
back in your purse at a moment's notice. Don't
worry, no one will notice!

Work in Double-Knitting for 10 (11) inches. For custom size, make tab 10 inches long.

Slip the dpn out of the sts; the knit tube will open.

Slip the front (knit) sts onto 1 dpn the back (purl) sts onto another dpn.

Hold the 2 dpns parallel and graft the sts tog using the Kitchener st (page 166).

FINISHING

Attach rings by sliding onto St st flap and folding flap to WS of belt. Sew neatly in place.

Stabilize the braid (optional): To keep the braided section of the belt from stretching out of shape while wearing, cut a piece of grosgrain ribbon the length of the braided section plus 2 inches. Fold under ½ inch on each end. Using coordinating sewing thread, sew folded ends of ribbon to double knit section of belt. Tack braid to ribbon at intervals as desired. ■

ORIENT EXPRESS EYE PILLOW

DESIGN BY DAWN LEESEMAN

WHAT'S IN THE BAG

Rowan Classic Yarns Pure Silk
  DK (DK weight; 100% silk,
  137 yds/50g per skein): 1 ball
  tranquil #00156
Size 5 (3.5mm) needles
Size 6 (4mm) needles or size needed to
  obtain gauge
100 #6 Czech glass beads in hematite
Size #10 steel crochet hook or size to fit
  through opening of bead
Size E/4 (3.5mm) crochet hook
Sewing needle
¼ yd fabric for lining
Thread to match fabric
1¼–1½ cups raw rice
Aromatherapy herbs or oils

SKILL LEVEL

 EASY

FINISHED SIZE

8½ x 4 inches

GAUGE

22 sts and 36 rows = 4 inches/10cm in beaded
Seed st with smaller needles.
22 sts and 32 rows = 4 inches/10cm in St st
with larger needles.
To save time, take time to check gauge.

SPECIAL ABBREVIATION

Place bead on next st and purl (PBP): Place a
bead onto steel crochet hook. With hook facing
you, insert the hook into the next st on LH
needle, pull the loop through the bead, replace
the st with bead onto the LH and purl.

PATTERN NOTES

It's a good idea to purchase extra beads
because some center holes may be misshapen.
When using eye pillow, keep non-beaded side
next to eyes.

BEADED PIECE

With smaller needles, cast on 47 sts.
Row 1 (RS): K1, *p1, k1; rep from * across.
Row 2: K1, *PBP, k1; rep from * across.
Row 3: K1, p1, k1; rep from * across.
Row 4: K1, PBP, k1, *p1, k1; rep from * to last
2 sts, PBP, k1.
  Rep Rows 3 and 4 until piece measures
4½ inches, ending with Row 4.
  Work Rows 1 and 2 once more.
  Bind off all sts in pat.

PLAIN PIECE

With larger needles, cast on 47 sts.
  Work in St st until piece measures 4½ inches.
  Bind off all sts.

ASSEMBLY

Weave in all ends.
  Place rice in a bowl, add desired herbs or
oils, set aside.
  Using knitted piece as template, cut 2 pieces
from lining fabric, each ½ inch wider and
longer than knitted piece. With RS of fabric tog
and beg on long side edge, using matching
thread, sew ¼-inch seam around 3 sides. Turn
right-side out and fill with scented rice; sew
across open end.
  With WS of St st and beaded pieces tog and
using larger crochet hook, beg at corner of
long side of rectangle, work sc through both
layers around 3 sides of the rectangle; insert
rice pouch; work sc across last side to close;
do not turn.
  Work 1 rnd reverse sc around all 4 sides,
fasten off. ■

"Just to make sure I'm not 'knit-less,' I always keep extra yarn and needles in tow just in case."

FANCIFUL FELTED PURSE

DESIGN BY PHYLLIS SANDFORD

WHAT'S IN THE BAG

Plymouth Galway Worsted (worsted weight; 100% wool; 210 yds/100g per ball): 2 balls purple #132 (A)

Plymouth Galway Worsted Highland Heather (worsted weight; 100% wool; 210 yds/100g per ball): 1 ball each green #728 (B) and blue-gray #732 (C)

Size 13 (9mm) needles or size needed to obtain gauge

Sharp sewing needle

Sewing thread to match yarn

Beads of choice

Beading thread

Beading needle

Large snap

SKILL LEVEL

■□□□ BEGINNER

FINISHED SIZE

10½ inches wide x 10 inches long

PRE-FELTING GAUGE

12 sts and 14 rows = 4 inches/10cm in St st. Exact gauge is not critical; make sure your sts are loose and airy.

PURSE

With A, cast on 136 sts.
Work in St st until piece measures approx 20 inches.
Bind off.
Fold fabric in half vertically.
With A, sew side and bottom seams.

LEAVES

With B, cast on 75 sts.
Work in St st until piece measures approx 6½ inches.
Bind off.

FLOWER

With C, cast on 75 sts.
Work in St st until piece measures approx 6½ inches.
Bind off.

STRAP

With A, cast on 80 sts.
Work 10 rows in St st.
Bind off.
With WS out and using A, sew cast-on and bound-off edges tog.
Turn right side out.

FELTING

Felt bag, strap, flower and leaf fabric following felting instructions on page 167. When bag reaches finished measurements or desired size, gently rinse all pieces in the sink. Roll the bag in a towel and squeeze out the excess water. Roll strap between your hands to shape. Let all pieces dry thoroughly.

ASSEMBLY

Sew ends of strap to inside of bag.

Cut 3 leaf shapes from the green fabric.

Cut 5 petal shapes and center circle for flower.

Arrange leaves, petals and flower center on front of bag as desired.

Using sharp needle and matching thread, referring to photo, sew to front of bag, starting with leaves and ending with center circle.

Using beads of choice, beading needle and beading thread, referring to photo, sew a row of beads along the top edge of the bag.

Sew 2nd row of beads approx 1 inch below first. Sew beads to leaves. Sew large bead in center of flower.

With sharp needle and thread, sew large snap to center of WS of bag, approx 1½ inches from top or positioned as desired. ■

Tip Keep a "knitting bag within a knitting bag". This is great for air travel. Since space is at a minimum, bring your mini bag on the plane, and keep a larger bag in your suitcase.

CHICO'S SWEATER

DESIGN BY SHIRLEY MACNULTY

WHAT'S IN THE BAG

Moda Dea Sassy Stripes (light worsted weight; 100% acrylic; 147 yds/50g per ball):1 ball swish #6952

Size 4 (3.5mm) straight and double-point needles (set of 4)

Size 5 (3.75mm) needles or size needed to obtain gauge

Small piece of contrasting yarn for a marker

SKILL LEVEL

◼◼◻◻ EASY

SIZE

Small, to fit a 2–4 pound miniature dog such as a miniature Chihuahua.

FINISHED MEASUREMENTS

Chest: 11 inches
Length: 11 inches

GAUGE

22 sts and 30 rows = 4 inches/10cm in St st with larger needles.
To save time, take time to check gauge.

SPECIAL ABBREVIATION

Make 1 (M1): Insert LH needle from front to back under the running thread between the last st worked and next st on RH needle; knit into the back of resulting loop.

PATTERN NOTE

This sweater begins at the neck.

SWEATER

With smaller needles, cast on 48 sts.

Work in K1, P1 Rib for 1½ inches, ending with a WS row.

Inc row (RS): With larger needles, k1, M1, knit to last st, M1, k1—50 sts.

Continue in St st rep Inc row [every other row] 3 more times, ending with a WS row—56 sts.

Leg openings

Row 1 (RS): K10, bind off 4 sts, k28, (this includes st rem from bind off), bind off 4 sts, k10 (this includes st rem from bind off).

131

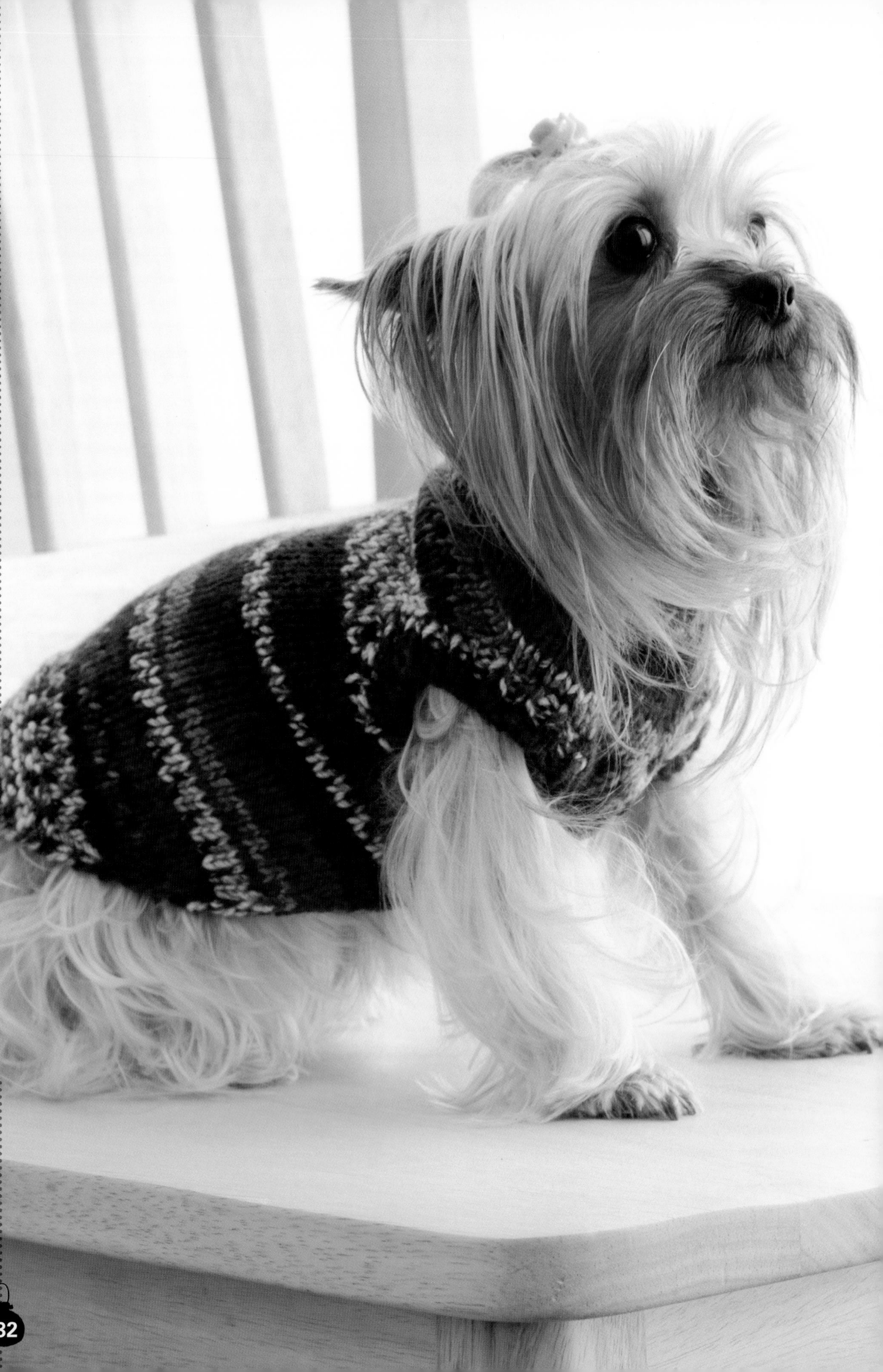

Row 2: Working all 3 sections at once, p10, attach 2nd ball of yarn, p28, attach 3rd ball of yarn, p10.

Row 3: First section: k1, M1, knit to last 3 sts, k2tog, k1; middle section: k1, ssk, knit to last 3 sts, k2tog, k1; last section: k1, ssk, knit to last st, M1, k1—10 sts in first and last sections, 26 sts in middle section.

Row 4: Purl.

Rep [Rows 3 and 4] twice—10 sts in first and last sections; 22 sts in middle section.

Work 4 rows even in St st.

Inc row (RS): First section: knit to last st, M1, k1; middle section: k1, M1, knit to last st, M1, k1; last section: k1, M1, knit to end—11 sts in first and last sections; 24 sts in middle section.

Continue in St st and rep Inc row [every RS row] twice more, ending with a WS row—13 sts in first and last sections, 28 sts in middle section.

Next row (join sections): K13, cast on 4 sts, knit across middle section, cast on 4 sts, knit to end—62 sts.

Next row: Purl.

Shape back

Row 1 (RS): K1, ssk, knit to last 3 sts, k2tog, k1—60 sts.

Row 2: K1, purl to last st, k1.

Row 3: Knit.

Row 4: Rep Row 2

Rep [Rows 1–4] 9 more times—42 sts.

Dec row (RS): K1, ssk, knit to last 3 sts, k2tog, k1—40 sts.

Next row: Knit.

Rep [last 2 rows] 9 more times—22 sts.

Bind off as to knit.

Leg ribbing

With dpn, pick up and knit 32 sts around leg opening, dividing sts onto 3 needles.

Work 5 rnds in K1, P1 Rib.

Bind off in rib.

Rep for other leg opening.

FINISHING

Block to finished measurements. Sew seam, beg at neck ribbing and end at back shaping. Weave in all ends. ■

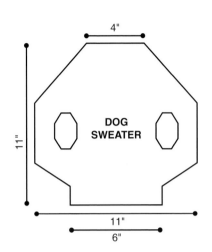

Tip With a small, compact purse, you can knit a stitch or two standing in line at the supermarket or even at a cocktail party!

FRILLY PRILLY PONCHO

DESIGN BY JEAN CLEMENT

WHAT'S IN THE BAG

Berroco Pure Merino Heather (worsted weight;100% extra fine merino wool; 92 yds/50g per ball): 3 balls Tyrolean Alps #8616(A)
Berroco Jasper (worsted weight; 100% fine merino wool; 98 yds/50g per hank): 3 hanks copper silk #3810 (B)
Size 9 (5.5mm) 16- and 24-inch circular needles or size needed to obtain gauge
Stitch markers, 1 in CC for beg of rnd
Stitch holders or waste yarn

(4 MEDIUM)

SKILL LEVEL
◼◼◼▢ INTERMEDIATE

SIZE
To fit medium-size dog (25–30 lbs)

FINISHED MEASUREMENTS
Neck circumference: approx 13 inches
Back length: approx 16 inches

GAUGE
20 sts and 30 rows = 4 inches/10cm in Navaho Basket stitch.
To save time, take time to check gauge.

PATTERN STITCHES
K3, P1 Rib (worked in rnd on multiple of 4 sts)
Rnd 1: K1, *p1, k3; rep from * to last 3 sts, p1, k2.
   Rep Rnd 1 for pat.

K3, P1 Rib (worked flat on multiple of 4 sts + 5)
Row 1 (WS): K1, p1, k1, *p3, k1; rep from * to last 2 sts, p1, k1.
Row 2 (RS): K2, *p1, k3; rep from * to last 3 sts, p1, k2.
   Rep Rows 1 and 2 for pat.

Stripe Pattern (in rib)
Work 4 rnds/rows A, 2 rnds/rows B, 2 rnds/rows A, 2 rnds/rows B.
   Rep these 10 rnds/rows for stripe pat.

Navaho Basket (multiple of 4 sts + 5)
Row 1 (RS): With A, knit.
Row 2 (WS): With A, purl.
Row 3: With B, k1, *k1, sl 1 wyif; rep from * last st, k1.
Row 4: With B, purl.
Row 5: With A, k1, *sl 1 wyif, k1; rep from * to last st, k1
Row 6: With A, purl.
Rows 7 and 9: With B, k2, *sl 1, k3; rep to last 3 sts, sl 1, k2.
Rows 8 and 10: With B, k1, p1, *sl 1, p3; rep to last 3 sts, sl 1, p1, k1.
Rows 11–16: Rep Rows 1-6.
Rows 17 and 19: With B, k1, *k3, sl 1; rep from * to last 4 sts, k4.
Rows 18 and 20: With B, k1, *p3, sl 1; rep from * to last 4 sts, p3, k1.
   Rep Rows 1–20 for pat.

PATTERN NOTES
Carry unused color up side edge, catching it every couple rounds to secure.

   The back length can be adjusted by working fewer or more, full or partial repeats of the Navaho Basket pattern. To determine the correct length for your dog, measure from the base of dog's back neck to hip bones. The shaping decreases for the dog's hind quarters should begin at hip bones. The body will also look best if the decreases are begun on Row 1 or 11 of the Navaho Basket pattern.

PONCHO
Collar and Front Panel
With shorter circular needle and A, cast on 64 sts; place marker for beg of rnd and join, taking care not to twist sts.

   Counting cast-on as first rnd of Stripe pat, work 20 rnds in Stripe pat, ending with A.

   Cut B, remove beg of rnd marker and turn to beg working back and forth.
Next row (WS): With A, work 45 sts in established rib, then place rem 19 sts on holder for back neck.

"We travel with our dogs in a 22-foot trailer, and I'm usually good about making sure my knitting projects stay safe. However, we once made a trip to Tennessee, and I wasn't so careful. When we arrived at our destination, we parked and visited friends. During our absence, one of the dogs jumped up onto the bathroom counter and somehow managed to turn the water faucet on. Of course, my knitting bag that had been sitting on the counter was now floating in the middle of the trailer. Since that day I've never let my knitting bag out of my sight!"

Continuing in established rib and Stripe pat, work 40 rows.

Cut B.

Next row (RS): With A, work in established pat.

Body

Change to longer needle.

Next row (RS): With RS facing and using A, pick up and knit 27 sts along left edge of front panel (approx 2 sts for every 3 rows), knit 19 sts from holder, pick up and knit 27 sts along right edge of front panel; place 45 front panel sts on holder—73 sts on needle.

Next row (WS): K1, purl to last st, k1.

Rejoin B and beg with Row 3, work in Navajo Basket pat until body measures 16 inches, ending with Row 10 or 20.

Set-up row (RS): Working in established pat, k19, k2tog, place marker, k31, place marker, ssk, k19—71 sts.

Next row: Work in established pat, purling the dec sts.

Dec row (RS): Work to 2 sts before marker, k2tog, slip marker, work 31 sts, slip marker, ssk, work to end—69 sts.

Rep Dec row [every RS row] 9 times, purling all dec sts on WS and ending on a RS row—51 sts.

Next row (WS, dec): Work to 2 sts before first marker, ssp, work center 31 sts, p2tog, work to end—49 sts.

Continue to dec [every row] 8 times—33 sts.

Border

Rnd 1 (RS): With A, k2, [p1, k3] 7 times, p1, k2; pick up 105 sts along body edge (approx 3 sts for every 4 rows), work 45 held front panel sts in established pat; pick up 105 sts along body

edge, place marker for beg of rnd and join—288 sts.

Work K3, P1 Rib as established for 8 rnds, alternating 2 rnds A and 2 rnds B, and *at the same time*, continue to dec every rnd at markers—272 sts.

With A, work 4 rnds even, then bind off in rib.

FINISHING

Weave in ends; block gently. ∎

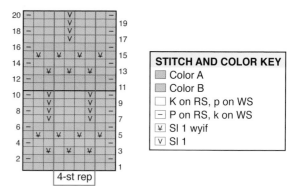

STITCH AND COLOR KEY

▨	Color A
▨	Color B
□	K on RS, p on WS
−	P on RS, k on WS
ⱴ	Sl 1 wyif
ⱱ	Sl 1

Note: Each row is worked with 1 color only. Use the color (A or B) that is the first color in row.

NAVAHO BASKET

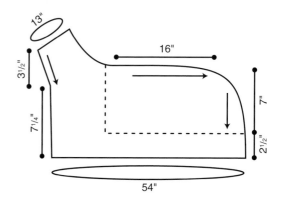

LUXURIOUS LACE COLLAR

DESIGN BY JOËLLE MEIER RIOUX FOR CLASSIC ELITE YARNS

WHAT'S IN THE BAG

Classic Elite Yarns Blithe (DK weight; 100% baby camel; 128 yds/25g per hank): 1 hank sage #C10459

Size 6 (4mm) needles or size needed to obtain gauge

Size E/4 (3.5mm) crochet hook

One 2-inch toggle button

SKILL LEVEL

■■■□ INTERMEDIATE

FINISHED SIZE

6 x 21 inches

GAUGE

23 sts and 28 rows = 4 inches/10cm in St st.
To save time, take time to check gauge.

SPECIAL ABBREVIATIONS

Decrease 3, left-leaning (Dec3L): Sl 1k, k3tog, psso.

Decrease 3, right-leaning (Dec3R): K3tog, sl st from RH back to LH needle and pass second st on LH needle over first. Sl st back to RH needle.

Decrease 4 (Dec4): Ssk, k3tog, pass 2nd st on RH needle over first st.

Knit 1 or make a bobble (k1/MB): Either k1 or make a bobble (see Pattern Notes).

Make Bobble (MB): Knit into the [front, back] twice, then front again of the same st; turn; p5, turn; k5, turn; p2tog, k1, ssp, turn; sk2p.

Place marker (pm): Place a marker on needle to separate pats.

PATTERN STITCHES

Right Edge Panel (5-st panel)
Row 1 (RS): Sl 1k, k2, yo, k2tog.
Row 2: Knit.
     Rep Rows 1 and 2 for pat.

Leaf Panel (13-st panel)
Row 1 (RS): [K1, yo] twice, Dec3L, yo, k1, yo, Dec3R, [yo, k1] twice.
Row 2 and all WS rows: Purl.
Row 3: K1, yo, k3, yo, Dec4, yo, k3, yo, k1.
Row 5: K1, yo, ssk, k1, k2tog, yo, k1, yo, ssk, k1, k2tog, yo, k1.
Row 7: K1, yo, ssk, k1, k2tog, yo, k1/MB, yo, ssk, k1, k2tog, yo, k1.
Row 8: Purl.
     Rep Rows 1–8 for pat.

Center Panel (7-st panel)
Row 1 (RS): K1, yo, k2tog, k2, yo, k2tog.
Row 2: Knit.
     Rep Rows 1 and 2 for pat.

Left Edge Panel (5-st panel)
Row 1 (RS): K1, yo, k2tog, k2.
Row 2: Sl 1k, k4.
     Rep Rows 1 and 2 for pat.

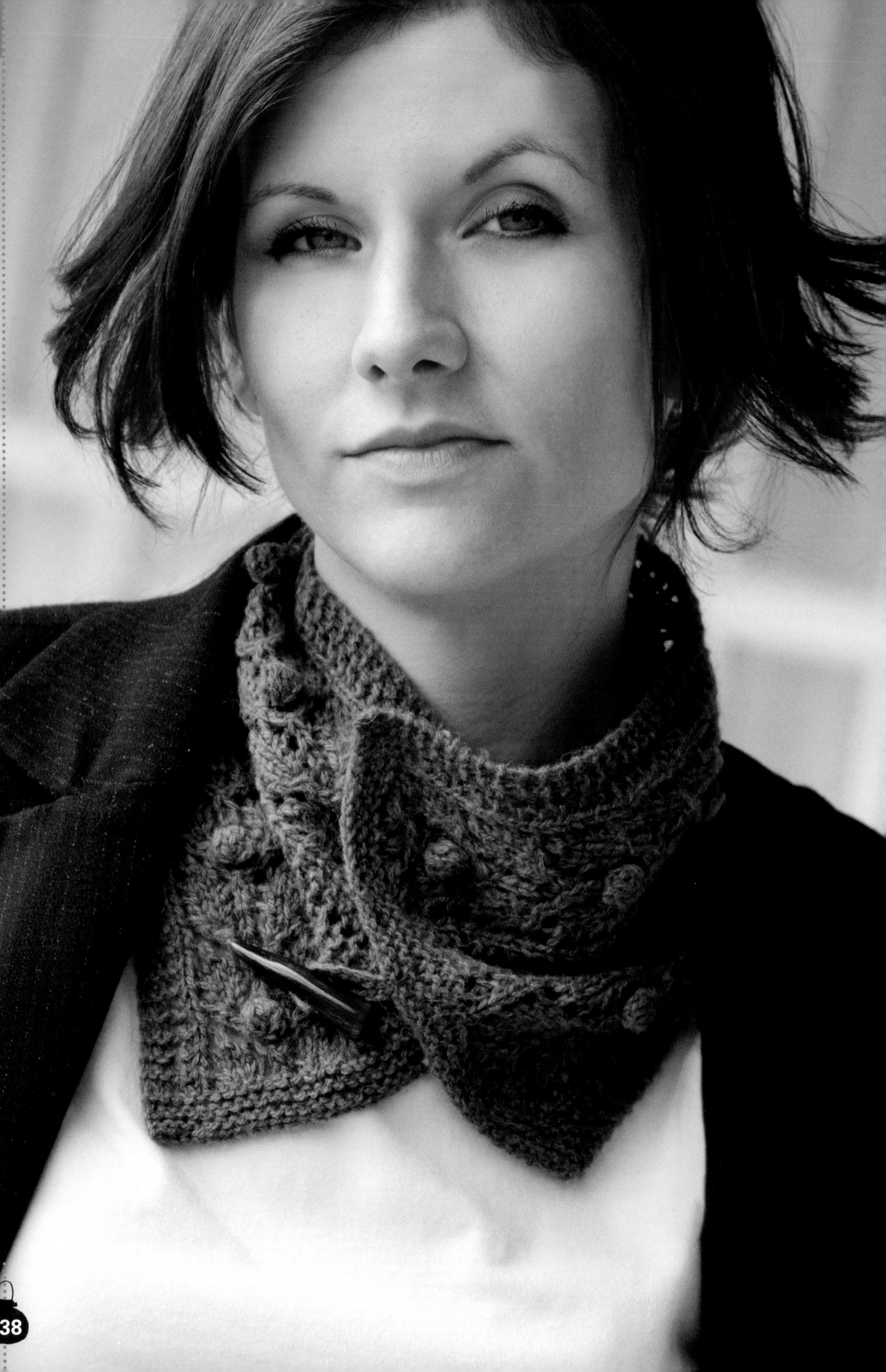

PATTERN NOTES

A bobble is worked every other Row 7 of Leaf Panels, alternating between the 2 panels; otherwise, knit the stitch.

Slip first stitch of every row as to knit.

A chart for the Leaf Panel is provided for those preferring to work from charts.

COLLAR

Cast on 43 sts.

Knit 6 rows.

Set-up row (WS): Sl 1, k4, p13, k7, p13, k5.

Establish pat (RS): Work Row 1 of Right Edge Panel, pm, work Row 1 of Leaf Panel, work Row 1 of Center Panel, pm, work Row 1 of Leaf Panel, pm, work Row 1 of Left Edge Panel.

Work even in established pats until piece measures 18½ inches from beg (measure garter st at center, not stretched), ending with Row 5 of Leaf Panel.

Knit 5 rows.

Bind off all sts as to knit.

FINISHING

Block to measurements, being careful not to flatten bobbles. With crochet hook, ch 15 and attach ends of chain to center panel on cast-on edge, forming a loop. Sew button to center panel on opposite end, approx 2 inches in from edge. ■

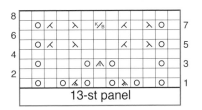

Tip Prepare a "knitting emergency travel kit" for your car. Purchase a small plastic case in which to keep your essentials. You can easily store this under a seat or in the trunk.

13-st panel

LEAF PANEL

STITCH KEY

☐ K on RS, p on WS

◌ Yo

Dec3L

Dec3R

Dec4

Ssk

K2tog

K1/MB

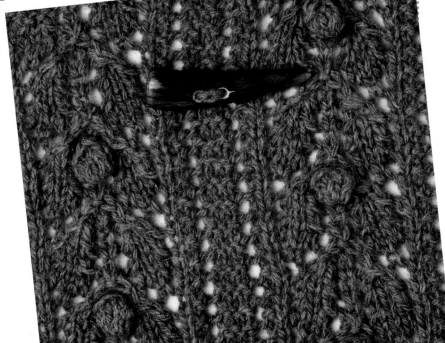

HOME ADORNMENTS

If you want to add some character to your abode, the creations to follow will be just what you've been searching for. So pack up that knitting bag you love with a "new favorite" today!

RUSTIC BASKET WEAVE TABLE RUNNER

DESIGN BY CELESTE PINHEIRO

WHAT'S IN THE BAG

Mission Falls 1824 Wool (worsted weight; 100% merino superwash; 85 yds/50g per ball): 3 balls each stone #002 (A), amethyst #023 (B) and curry #013 (C); 2 balls each russet #010 (D), thyme #016 (E) and denim #021 (F)

Size 8 (5mm) needles or size needed to obtain gauge

SKILL LEVEL

 BEGINNER

FINISHED SIZE

14 x 90 inches

GAUGE

19 sts and 26 rows = 4 inches/10cm in Basket Weave pat.

To save time, take time to check gauge.

PATTERN STITCH

Basket Weave (multiple of 8 sts + 3)
Rows 1 and 3 (WS): K4, *p3, k5; rep from * to last 7 sts, p3, k4.

Row 2 (RS): P4, *k3, p5; rep from * to last 7 sts, k3, p4.
Row 4: Knit.
Rows 5 and 7: *P3, k5; rep from * to last 3 sts, p3.
Row 6: *K3, p5; rep from * to last 3 sts, k3.
Row 8: Knit.
  Rep Rows 1–8 for pat.

PATTERN NOTE

A chart of the Basket Weave pattern is provided for those preferring to work from chart.

TABLE RUNNER

With A, using long-tail method, cast on 69 sts.
Row 1 (WS): K1, work Basket Weave pat to last st, k1.

  Maintaining first and last st in garter st, continue Basket Weave pat, and *at the same time*, work stripe pat as follows: 1 more row A, 8 rows E, 20 rows B, 12 rows C, 4 rows F, 12 rows A, 4 rows D, 8 rows B, 20 rows E, 4 rows F, 12 rows C, 12 rows A, 8 rows B, 20 rows D, 4 rows E, 12 rows C, 4 rows F, 12 rows A, 4 rows D, 8 rows E, 20 rows B, 4 rows F, 12 rows C,12 rows A, 8 rows E, 4 rows D, 20 rows F,

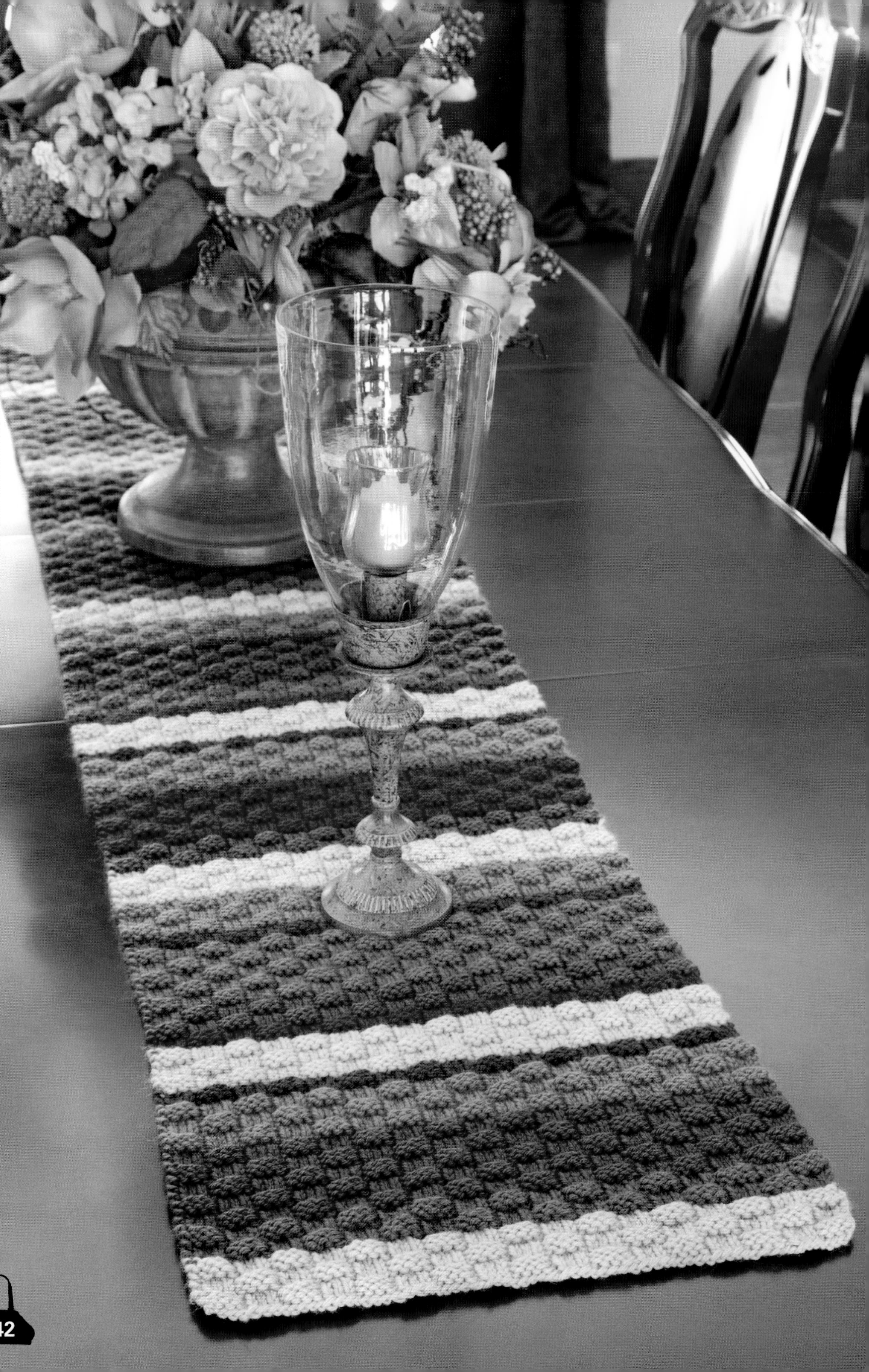

"When traveling, I like to work on projects that call for a variegated yarn. It's fun to see the gradual flow of one color after another, creating a surprising pattern. If I'm in the car, I don't have to glance down so much—and I don't get car sick either!"

4 rows B, 12 rows E (center stripe), 4 rows B,
20 rows F, 4 rows D, 8 rows E, 12 rows A,
12 rows C, 4 rows F, 20 rows B, 8 rows E,
4 rows D, 12 rows A, 4 rows F, 12 rows C,
4 rows E, 20 rows D, 8 rows B, 12 rows A,
12 rows C, 4 rows F, 20 rows E, 8 rows B,
4 rows D, 12 rows A, 4 rows F, 12 rows C,
20 rows B, 8 rows E, 12 rows A.
   Bind off with A.
   Weave in ends. Block as necessary. ∎

STITCH KEY
☐ K on RS, p on WS
⊟ P on RS, k on RS

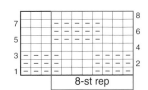

BASKET WEAVE

PRETTY PASTELS LAP BLANKET

DESIGN BY KATHARINE HUNT

WHAT'S IN THE BAG

Plymouth Encore Worsted (worsted weight; 75% acrylic/25% wool; 200 yds/100g per ball): 4 balls off-white #240 (A); 1 ball each green #1232 (B), light purple #958 (C), rust #456 (D), and earth #6002 (E)

Size 8 (5mm) needles or size needed to obtain gauge

Size E/4 (3.5mm) crochet hook

SKILL LEVEL

 INTERMEDIATE

FINISHED SIZE

Approx 40 x 41 inches

GAUGE

24 sts and 26 rows = 4 inches/10cm over Cable panel.
To save time, take time to check gauge.

BLANKET

Cable Panel
Make 5

With A, cast on 21 sts.
Work Cable Panel chart for 260 rows (13 reps).
Bind off.

Zigzag Panel 1
Make 2

With B (D), cast on 31 sts.
Work Zigzag Panel chart for 260 rows (13 reps).
Bind off.

Zigzag Panel 2
Make 2

With C (E), cast on 31 sts.
Beg on Row 11, work Zigzag Panel chart for 260 rows (13 reps).
Bind off.

FINISHING

Sew panels tog in following color order: A, B, A, C, A, D, A, E, A.
Weave in all ends.
Block blanket lightly to measurements.

EDGING

With crochet hook and A, work 2 rows of sc across top of blanket, fasten off.
Rep on bottom edge. ∎

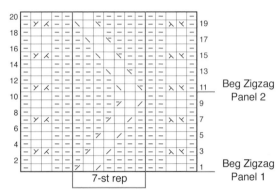

Tip Never dig down to the bottom of your bag again for that long lost tape measure! Keep your knitting essentials in a clear makeup bag for easy access.

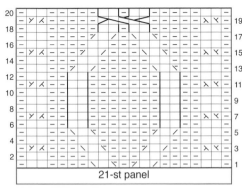

CABLE PANEL

21-st panel

ZIGZAG PANEL

7-st rep

Beg Zigzag Panel 2

Beg Zigzag Panel 1

STITCH KEY

- ⊟ P on RS, k on WS
- ☐ K on RS, p on WS
- Sl 1 to cn and hold in back, k1, k1 from cn
- Sl 1 to cn and hold in front, k1, k1 from cn
- Sl 2 to cn and hold in front, p1, k2 from cn
- Sl 1 to cn and hold in back, k2, p1 from cn
- Sl 2 to cn and hold in front, k3, k2 from cn

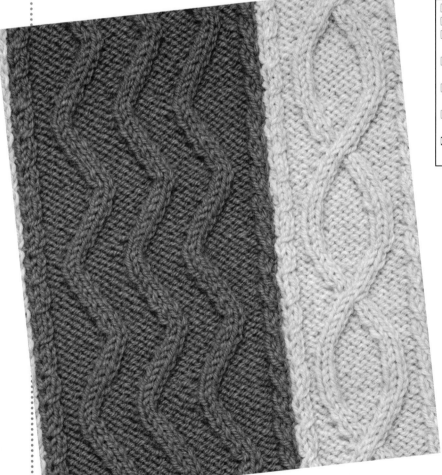

LACED-UP CABLES AFGHAN

DESIGN BY SUZANNE ATKINSON

WHAT'S IN THE BAG

Plymouth Galway Chunky
  (bulky weight; 100% wool;
  123 yds/100g per ball): 13
  balls maroon #12 (A), 11 balls
  charcoal gray #704 (B), 3 balls olive
  heather #750 (C)
Size 10 (6.mm) needles
Size I/9 (5.5mm) crochet hook
Cable needle

SKILL LEVEL
■■□□ EASY

FINISHED MEASUREMENTS
52 x 64 inches

GAUGE
22 sts and 22 rows = 4¾ inches/12cm in
Cable Pat (i.e. width of one cable panel).
To save time, take time to check gauge.

SPECIAL ABBREVIATIONS
Cable 6 Forward (C6F): Sl next 3 sts to cn
and hold in front, k3, k3 from cn.
Make 1 (M1): Insert LH needle from
front to back under the running thread
between the last st worked and next
st on RH needle; knit into the back of
resulting loop.

PATTERN STITCH
Cable Panel (22-st panel)
Row 1 (RS): K5, p3, k6, p3, k5.
Row 2: K8, p6, k8.
Row 3: K2, yo, ssk, k1, p3, C6F, p3, k1,
k2tog, yo, k2.
Row 4: Rep Row 2.
  Rep Rows 1–4 for pat.

PATTERN NOTES
Afghan is worked as separate cable
panels; the panels are joined by
lacing crocheted chains through
eyelets in the panels and joining at ends.
  A chart for the Cable Panel is provided for
those preferring to work from charts.

AFGHAN
Make 11 Cable Panels (6 in A and 5 in B)
  Cast on 20 sts.
  Knit 2 rows.
Next row: K2, yo, ssk, k12, k2tog, yo, k2.
  Knit 2 rows.
Next row: K9, M1, k2, M1, k9—22 sts.
  Work [Rows 1–4 of Cable pat] 49 times,
ending with Row 4.
Next row: K8, k2tog, k2, k2tog, k8—20 sts.
  Knit 3 rows.

Next row: K2, yo, ssk, k12, k2tog, yo, k2.
Next row: Knit.
  Bind off.

FINISHING

Weave in all ends. Block cable panels.
  With crochet hook and C, make 22 8-ft lengths of chain st.
  Lay cable panels side by side on large flat surface alternating colors (A, B, A, B, etc. ending with A).
  Using crocheted chains, join adjacent panels as for lacing sneakers, using 2 crochet chains for each join, beg at first eyelet in each panel and alternating eyelets to end of panel. Let 8 inches of each crochet chain extend beyond afghan for tying together in a bow at each end of afghan.
  Weave single crocheted chain through eyelets at each side panel edge as follows: *pull chain through first eyelet from RS to WS; go around outer edge, then pull chain from RS to WS through next eyelet; rep from * to end (see photo). ■

Tip When working with multiple colors of yarn, instead of traveling with large unnecessary skeins, wind off small balls of only the colors you'll need.

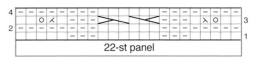

CABLE PANEL

22-st panel

STITCH KEY
- ☐ K on RS, p on WS
- ⊟ P on RS, k on WS
- ⊡ Yo
- ⊠ Ssk
- ⊡ K2tog
- C6F

SPIRALED I-CORD SEAT COVER

DESIGN BY SHIRLEY MACNULTY

WHAT'S IN THE BAG

Trendsetter Yarns Viva (bulky
  yarn; 65% new wool/20%
  acrylic/15% polyamide; 55
  yds/50g per skein): 6 skeins
  cask & cleaver #814

Size 13 (9mm) 16 inch circular needle
  or size needed to obtain gauge
Size K (6.5mm) crochet hook

SKILL LEVEL

■■□□ EASY

FINISHED SIZE

Diameter: Approx 17½ inches
(including edging)

GAUGE

12 sts and 12 rnds = 4 inches/10cm in St st in
an I-cord tube.
To save time, take time to check gauge.

PATTERN NOTES

Most of pattern is worked as a 4-stitch I-cord;
at the very end, it is gradually decreased to
1 stitch.

Each skein of the designated yarn yields
approximately 2¼ yards of I-cord.

Some may find it easier to sew the I-cord
together as they knit, sewing after every
12 inches or so, then resuming knitting.

SEAT COVER

Cast on 4 sts.

Rnd 1: K4, do not turn; slide sts to opposite end
of needle pulling yarn tightly behind work.

Rep Rnd 1 until cord measures approx
12 yds or desired length.

Next rnd: K1, k2tog, k1—3 sts.

Next 3 rnds: Work as for Rnd 1 on 3 sts.

Next rnd: K2tog, k1.

Next 3 rnds: Work as for Rnd 1 on 2 sts.

Next rnd: K2tog.

Next 3 rnds: Work as for Rnd 1 on 1 st.

Fasten off.

FINISHING

Thread tapestry needle with an 18-inch piece
of project yarn.

With RS facing, and beg at cast-on end,
sew I-cord into a round flat coil using whip
st, catching 1 st on each side of the I-cord
tube. You should have 2 knit sts (1 from
each section of I-cord being sewn tog)
traveling tog in a straight line around
the top side of the piece. Every few sts,
skip 1 of the sts on the outer I-cord so
that the cover will lie flat. Add new
sewing yarn as necessary.

When finished sewing, work 1
rnd of dc around outside edge.

Weave loose ends into I-cord
tubes.

Wet-block piece, pulling it as
necessary to get it to lie flat. Put
between towels and cover with
heavy weights (such as large
books). Allow to dry thoroughly. ■

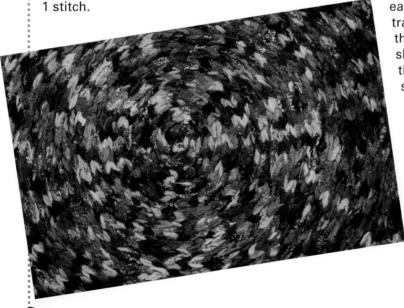

"Once many years ago, we were out in our little boat. We suddenly came to a stop, and lo and behold we got stranded on a sandbar. Luckily I had some knitting with me—we had to wait three hours for the rising tide to set us free!"

KNIT, THEN WEAVE, PLACE MATS

DESIGN BY COLLEEN SMITHERMAN

WHAT'S IN THE BAG

Lily Sugar 'n Cream (worsted weight; 100% cotton; 120 yds/71g per skein): 1 skein each cornflower blue #00083 (A) and soft ecru #01004 (B)

Size 8 (5mm) 29-inch circular needle

Size 11 (8mm) needles or size needed to obtain gauge

Size N/15 (10mm) crochet hook

5 stitch holders

SKILL LEVEL

■■□□ EASY

FINISHED SIZE

Approx 12½ x 17½ inches, not including fringe

GAUGE

14 sts and 15 rows = 4 inches/10cm in St st with larger needles (before weaving).
17 sts and 13 rows = 4 inches/10cm (after weaving).
To save time, take time to check gauge.

SPECIAL TECHNIQUE

Provisional Cast-On: With crochet hook and waste yarn, make a chain several sts longer than desired cast-on. With knitting needle and project yarn, pick up indicated number of sts in the "bumps" on back of chain.

When indicated in pattern, "unzip" the crochet chain to free live sts.

PATTERN NOTE

Each place mat is made from 5 narrow knit panels which are joined by weaving horizontal stripes across all 5 panels.

PLACE MAT

Panels
Make 5 (3 with A, 2 with B)
Using provisional method and A, cast on 15 sts.
Work 41 rows of St st.
Cut yarn and put sts on holder.

Weave panels together
With RS facing and cast-on edges at the bottom, lay panels side by side in the following sequence: A, B, A, B, A.
Thread yarn needle with A; do not cut yarn.

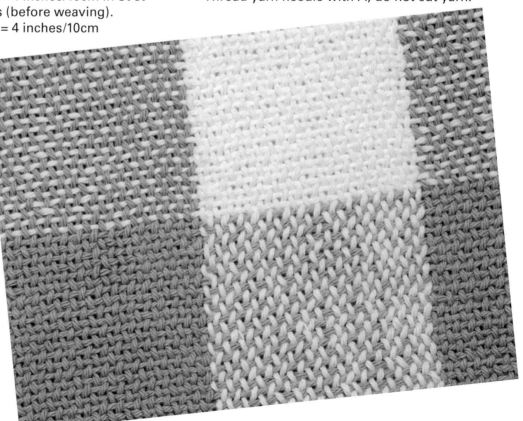

Beg with the bottom row and working to top row, work 2 rows of weaving through each row of knitting as described below:

*Beg at the outer A panel (right side if right-handed, left side if left-handed), weave needle and yarn horizontally across the knit row going under the left leg of every st, connecting all 5 panels as you weave; cut yarn, leaving a 3-inch tail at each side edge.

Thread the needle again, and weave needle and yarn across the same row again, going under the right leg of every st; cut yarn, leaving a 3-inch tail at each side edge.

Smooth out the weaving after each row so the width measures 17½ inches and weaving is uniform.

Rep from *, weaving twice in each row of knitting, creating stripes as follows: with A, weave 26 more rows through 13 rows of knitting; with B, weave 28 rows through 14 rows of knitting; with A, weave 28 rows through 14 rows of knitting.

Top border
Transfer sts from all holders to smaller needle—75 sts.

Tip Always keep a small magnifying glass on hand. This makes it easy to check your work closely when needed, and it is especially useful when working in less than ideal lighting.

With RS facing and using A, bind off all sts kwise.

Bottom border
Unzip Provisional Cast-On from each panel and transfer all live sts to smaller needle.

With RS facing and using A, bind off all sts kwise.

FINISHING
Weave in all knitting tails to WS.

Steam lightly, squaring up corners and sides.

Using overhand knots, tie weaving yarn tails tog 2 at a time close to place mat edges.

Trim fringe to 1 inch on both sides. ■

EARTH TONES AFGHAN

DESIGN BY PAULINE SCHULTZ

WHAT'S IN THE BAG

Patons SWS (worsted weight; 70% wool/30%soy; 110 yds/80g per ball): 15 balls natural earth #70013

Size 9 (5.5mm) needles or size needed to obtain gauge
Latch hook or large crochet hook
Stitch markers

SKILL LEVEL

◼◼☐☐ EASY

FINISHED SIZE

Approx 43 x 60 inches

GAUGE

15 sts and 18 rows = 4 inches/10cm Indian Cross pat.
To save time, take time to check gauge.

SPECIAL TECHNIQUE

Crochet Cast-On: Make slip knot on crochet hook. *Hold crochet hook vertically in front of and at right angles to the needle with the needle point facing right. Take the yarn under the needle, up and across the front of the crochet hook. Pull yarn through loop—new st on needle. Rep from * as required. Slip loop from crochet hook to needle to form the last st.

SPECIAL ABBREVIATIONS

Knit 1 with 4 Wraps (K1W4): Insert needle into next st and wrap yarn loosely 4 times around the needle, then knit the st.
Cross 8 Left (C8L): Sl 8 pwise, dropping all extra wraps (8 long sts result); insert LH needle into the 2nd 4 of these 8 long sts and pass them to the left over the first 4 (4 sts on LH needle,

4 sts on RH needle); sl 4 sts from RH back to LH needle; knit the 8 crossed sts.
Cross 4 Left (C4L): Sl 4 pwise dropping all extra wraps (4 long sts result); insert LH needle into the 2nd 2 of these 4 long sts and pass them to the left over the first 2 (2 sts on LH needle and 2 sts on RH needle); sl 2 sts from RH to LH needle; knit the 4 crossed sts.
Place marker (pm): Place a marker on needle to separate pats.

PATTERN STITCH

Indian Cross (multiple of 8 sts)
Rows 1–4: Knit.
Row 5: K1W4 in each st.
Row 6: [C8L] 4 times.
Rows 7–10: Knit.
Row 11: Rep Row 5.
Row 12: C4L, [C8L] 3 times, C4L.
Rep Rows 1–12 for pat.

AFGHAN

Left Panel

Crochet cast on 39 sts.
Knit 3 rows.
Set-up pat (RS): K5, pm, work 32 sts in Indian Cross pat, pm, k2.
Working edge sts in garter st and sts between markers in Indian Cross pat, work 25 reps of Indian Cross, then work Rows 1–6 of pat once more.
Knit 6 rows.
Bind off as to purl to last st, place this st on waste yarn for holder; cut yarn leaving a 6-inch tail and draw through next to last st.

Right Panel

Crochet cast on 39 sts.
Knit 3 rows.
Set-up pat (RS): K2, pm, work 32 sts in Indian Cross pat, pm, k5.
Work as for left panel to bind-off.
Slip first st to waste yarn for holder, bind off rem sts as to purl; cut yarn, leaving a 6-inch tail.

Center Panels
Make 2

Crochet cast on 36 sts.
Knit 3 rows.
Set-up pat (RS): K2, pm, work 32 sts in Indian Cross pat, pm, k2.
Work as for left panel to bind-off.
Slip first st to holder, bind off sts to last st, place this st on waste yarn for holder; cut yarn leaving a 6-inch tail and draw through next to last st.

FINISHING

Weave in all ends, except for the 3 (6-inch) tails.
Unravel sts on holders down through cast-on row.
Wet block each panel to measure

Tip Just roll up the strip you're working on, secure it with a needle or long stitch holder and away you go. You can even stash an extra ball of yarn inside!

10 x 60 inches (not including the side loops), using pins or blocking wires threaded through side loops to keep them straight.

When pieces are dry, join right panel to center panel using a crochet or latch hook as follows: insert hook through bottom left-side center panel loop; *catch the bottom loop of the right panel and draw through loop on hook; catch next center panel loop and draw through loop on hook; rep from * until last loop is on hook, then thread the 6-inch bind-off tail through it and fasten off securely.

Join rem panels as above. ∎

LUXEMBOURG LACE PLACE MATS

DESIGN BY CHRISTINE L. WALTER

WHAT'S IN THE BAG

Knit One Crochet Too 2nd Time Cotton (worsted weight; 75% recycled cotton/25% acrylic; 180 yds/100g per skein): 1 skein ochre #485

Size 8 (5mm) 24-inch circular needle or size needed to obtain gauge

SKILL LEVEL

◼◼◼◻◻ EASY

FINISHED SIZE

Approx 13½ x 17 inches

GAUGE

16 sts and 26 rows = 4 inches/10cm in combination of garter st and lace pat.
To save time, take time to check gauge.

SPECIAL ABBREVIATION

Place marker (pm): Place a marker on needle to separate pats.

PATTERN STITCH

Lace Pat (9-st panel)
Row 1 (RS): K1, [k2tog, yo] 3 times, k2.
Row 2: Purl.
Row 3: K2, [k2tog, yo] twice, k3.
Row 4: Purl.
 Rep Rows 1–4 for pat.

PLACE MAT

Cast on 55 sts.
 Knit 7 rows.
Next row: K5, pm, k9, pm, [k3, pm, k9, pm] 3 times, k5.
Set-up row (RS): Slipping markers, k5, work Lace pat over next 9 sts, [k3, work Lace pat over next 9 sts] 3 times, k5.

Continue pats as established, working 5 edge sts and 3 sts between each lace panel in garter st, until piece measures 16 inches, ending with Row 3 of lace pat.
 Removing markers on first row, knit 8 rows.
 Bind off very loosely on WS.

FINISHING

Weave in ends. Block as necessary. ■

Tip Take your knitting for a walk—place a small project, a short circular needle and a small ball of yarn in your fanny pack, and get moving!

It's in the Bag Home Adornments

BAMBOO BATH MAT

DESIGN BY CECILY GLOWIK MACDONALD

WHAT'S IN THE BAG

Classic Elite Wool Bam Boo (DK
weight; 50% wool/50% bamboo;
118 yds/50g per ball): 5 balls
each artichoke green #1672 (A)
and celery #1681 (B); 1 ball sachet
#1605 (C)
Size 10 (6mm) needles or size needed to
obtain gauge

3 LIGHT

SKILL LEVEL

 EASY

FINISHED SIZE

18 inches x 24 inches

PRE-FELTED GAUGE

16 sts and 24 rows = 4 inches/10cm in garter st
with 2 strands held tog.
To save time, take time to check gauge.

PATTERN NOTES

Bath mat is made of 9 separate rectangles of
one size and 9 separate rectangles of another
size that are then sewn together before felting.
All pieces are worked with 2 strands of yarn
held together.

BATH MAT

Large Rectangles
Make 9
With 1 strand each of A and B held tog, cast
on 25 sts.

Knit 44 rows.
Bind off.

Small Rectangles
Make 9
With 1 strand each of A and B held tog, cast
on 25 sts.
Knit 20 rows.
Bind off.

ASSEMBLY
Panels
Make 3
With tapestry needle and double-strand of C,
whip stitch the pieces tog so that seam sts are
visible.

*Sew the bound-off edge of a small
rectangle to the cast-on edge of a large
rectangle; sew the bound-off edge of the
large rectangle just used to the cast-on edge
of a new small rectangle; rep from * once,
then sew the bound-off edge of the last small
rectangle used to the cast-on edge of 1 more
large rectangle.

With tapestry needle and double-strand of B,
sew panels together along the long sides; the
middle panel is sewn
in facing the opposite
direction of the 2 side
panels (see Diagram).
Weave in ends.

FELTING
Follow basic felting
instructions on page
167 until finished
measurements are
obtained or piece is
desired size. Tumble dry
low, remove when still
damp. Shape and lay
flat to dry. ■

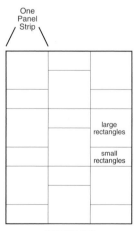

One Panel Strip

large rectangles

small rectangles

DIAGRAM

Tip Create knitting needle "bouquets"
by placing your needles in
decorative vases and tins around
the house. This not only adds character to
your surroundings, but it will be easy to grab
your needles and head out the door.

GENERAL INFORMATION

STANDARD ABBREVIATIONS

[ ] work instructions within brackets as many times as directed

( ) work instructions within parentheses in the place directed

** repeat instructions between the asterisks as directed

* repeat instructions following the single asterisk as directed

approx approximately

beg begin/beginning

CC contrasting color

ch chain stitch

cm centimeter(s)

cn cable needle

dec decrease/ decreases/ decreasing

dpn(s) double-point needle(s)

g gram

inc increase/increases/ increasing

k knit

k2tog knit 2 stitches together

LH left hand

lp(s) loop(s)

m meter(s)

M1 make one stitch

MC main color

mm millimeter(s)

oz ounce(s)

p purl

pat(s) pattern(s)

p2tog purl 2 stitches together

psso pass slipped stitch over

rem remain/remaining

rep repeat(s)

rev St st reverse stockinette stitch

RH right hand

rnd(s) rounds

RS right side

skp slip, knit, pass stitch over—one stitch decreased

sk2p slip 1, knit 2 together, pass slip stitch over the knit 2

together; 2 stitches have been decreased

sl slip

sl 1k slip 1 knitwise

sl 1p slip 1 purlwise

sl st slip stitch(es)

ssk slip, slip, knit these 2 stitches together—a decrease

ssp slip, slip, purl these 2 stitches together through the back loops [or tbl]—a decrease

st(s) stitch(es)

St st stockinette stitch/ stocking stitch

tbl through back loop(s)

tog together

WS wrong side

wyib with yarn in back

wyif with yarn in front

yd(s) yard(s)

yfwd yarn forward

yo yarn over

STANDARD YARN WEIGHT SYSTEM

Categories of yarn, gauge ranges and recommended needle sizes

Yarn Weight Symbol & Category Names	1 SUPER FINE	2 FINE	3 LIGHT	4 MEDIUM	5 BULKY	6 SUPER BULKY
Type of Yarns in Category	Sock, Fingering, Baby	Sport, Baby	DK, Light Worsted	Worsted, Afghan, Aran	Chunky, Craft, Rug	Bulky, Roving
Knit Gauge* Ranges in Stockinette Stitch to 4 inches	21–32 sts	23–26 sts	21–24 sts	16–20 sts	12–15 sts	6–11 sts
Recommended Needle in Metric Size Range	2.25–3.25mm	3.25–3.75mm	3.75–4.5mm	4.5–5.5mm	5.5–8mm	8mm
Recommended Needle U.S. Size Range	1 to 3	3 to 5	5 to 7	7 to 9	9 to 11	11 and larger

* GUIDELINES ONLY: The above reflect the most commonly used gauges and needle sizes for specific yarn categories.

SKILL LEVELS

BEGINNER

Projects for first-time knitters using basic knit and purl stitches. Minimal shaping.

EASY

Projects using basic stitches, repetitive stitch patterns, simple color changes and simple shaping and finishing.

INTERMEDIATE

Projects with a variety of stitches, such as basic cables and lace, simple intarsia, double-point needles and knitting in the round needle techniques, mid-level shaping and finishing.

EXPERIENCED

Projects using advanced techniques and stitches, such as short rows, Fair Isle, more intricate intarsia, cables, lace patterns and numerous color changes.

INCHES INTO MILLIMETERS & CENTIMETERS (Rounded off slightly)

inches	mm	cm	inches	cm	inches	cm	inches	cm
1/8	3	0.3	5	12.5	21	53.5	38	96.5
1/4	6	0.6	5 1/2	14	22	56	39	99
3/8	10	1	6	15	23	58.5	40	101.5
1/2	13	1.3	7	18	24	61	41	104
5/8	15	1.5	8	20.5	25	63.5	42	106.5
3/4	20	2	9	23	26	66	43	109
7/8	22	2.2	10	25.5	27	68.5	44	112
1	25	2.5	11	28	28	71	45	114.5
1 1/4	32	3.2	12	30.5	29	73.5	46	117
1 1/2	38	3.8	13	33	30	76	47	119.5
1 3/4	45	4.5	14	35.5	31	79	48	122
2	50	5	15	38	32	81.5	49	124.5
2 1/2	65	6.5	16	40.5	33	84	50	127
3	75	7.5	17	43	34	86.5		
3 1/2	90	9	18	46	35	89		
4	100	10	19	48.5	36	91.5		
4 1/2	115	11.5	20	51	37	94		

KNITTING NEEDLES CONVERSION CHART

U.S.	0	1	2	3	4	5	6	7	8	9	10	10 1/2	11	13	15
Metric(mm)	2	2 1/4	2 3/4	3 1/4	3 1/2	3 3/4	4	4 1/2	5	5 1/2	6	6 1/2	8	9	10

CROCHET HOOKS CONVERSION CHART

U.S.	1/B	2/C	3/D	4/E	5/F	6/G	8/H	9/I	10/J	10 1/2/K	N
Continental(mm)	2.25	2.75	3.25	3.5	3.75	4.25	5	5.5	6	6.5	9.0

GLOSSARY

bind-off—used to finish an edge

cast-on—process of making foundation stitches used in knitting

decrease—means of reducing the number of stitches in a row

increase—means of adding to the number of stitches in a row

intarsia—method of knitting a multicolored pattern into the fabric

knitwise—insert needle into stitch as if to knit

make 1—method of increasing using the strand between the last stitch worked and the next stitch

place marker—placing a purchased marker or loop of contrasting yarn onto the needle for ease in working a pattern repeat

purlwise—insert needle into stitch as if to purl

right side—side of garment or piece that will be seen when worn

selvage (selvedge) stitch—edge stitch used to make seaming easier

slip, slip, knit—method of decreasing by moving stitches from left needle to right needle and working them together

slip stitch—an unworked stitch slipped from left needle to right needle, usually as if to purl

wrong side—side that will be inside when garment is worn

work even—continue to work in the pattern as established without working any increases or decreases

work in pattern as established—continue to work following the pattern stitch as it has been set up or established on the needle, working any increases or decreases in such a way that the established pattern remains the same

yarn over—method of creating a stitch by wrapping the yarn over the right needle without working a stitch

BASIC STITCHES

Garter Stitch

When working back and forth, knit every row. When working in the round on circular or double-point needles, knit one round then purl one round.

Stockinette Stitch

When working back and forth, knit right-side rows and purl wrong-side rows. When working in the round on circular or double-point needles, knit all rounds.

Reverse Stockinette Stitch

When working back and forth, purl right-side rows and knit wrong-side rows. When working in the round on circular or double-point needles, purl all rounds.

Ribbing

Ribbing combines knit and purl stitches within a row to give stretch to the garment. Ribbing is most often used for the lower edge of the front and back, the cuffs and neck edge of garments.

The rib pattern is established on the first row. On subsequent rows the knit stitches are knitted and purl stitches are purled to form the ribs.

READING PATTERN INSTRUCTIONS

Before beginning a pattern, read through it to make sure you are familiar with the abbreviations that are used.

Some patterns may be written for more than one size. In this case the smallest size is given first, and others are placed in parentheses. When only one number is given, it applies to all sizes.

You may wish to highlight the numbers for the size you are making before beginning. It is also helpful to place a self-adhesive sheet on the pattern to note any changes made while working the pattern.

MEASURING

To measure pieces, lay them flat on a smooth surface. Take the measurement in the middle of the piece. For example, measure the length to the armhole in the center of the front or back piece, not along the outer edge where the edges tend to curve or roll.

GAUGE

The single most important factor in determining the finished size of a knit item is the gauge. Although not as important for flat, one-piece items, it is important when making a clothing item that needs to fit properly.

It is important to make a stitch gauge swatch at least 4 inches square with recommended patterns and needles before beginning.

Measure the swatch. If the number of stitches and rows are fewer than indicated under "Gauge" in the pattern, your needles are too large. Try another swatch with smaller-size needles. If the number of stitches and rows is more than indicated under "Gauge" in the pattern, your needles are too small. Try another swatch with larger-size needles.

Continue to adjust needle sizes until correct gauge is achieved.

WORKING FROM CHARTS

When working with more than one color or combination of stitches in a row, sometimes a chart is provided to help follow the pattern. On the chart each square represents one stitch. A key is given indicating the color or stitch represented by each color or symbol in the box.

When working in rows, odd-numbered rows are usually read from right to left and even-numbered rows from left to right.

For color-work charts, rows beginning at the right represent the right side of the work and are usually knit. Rows beginning at the left represent the wrong side and are usually purled.

When working in rounds, every row on the chart is a right-side row and is read from right to left.

USE OF ZERO

In patterns that include various sizes, zeros are sometimes necessary. For example, k0 (0,1) means if you are making the smallest or middle size, you would do nothing, and if you are making the largest size, you would k1.

INTARSIA

In certain patterns there are larger areas of color within the piece. Since this type of pattern requires a new color only for that section, it is not necessary to carry the yarn back and forth across the back. For this type of color change, a separate ball of yarn or bobbin is used for each color, making the yarn available only where needed. Bring the new yarn being used up and around the yarn just worked; this will "lock" the colors and prevent holes from occurring at the join.

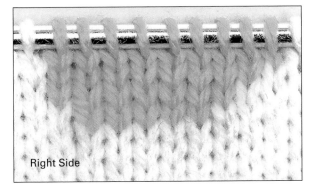

Right Side

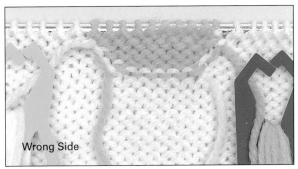

Wrong Side

SEAM FINISHES
Mattress Seam

This type of seam can be used for vertical seams (like side seams). It is worked with the right sides of the pieces facing you, making it easier to match stitches for stripe patterns. It is worked between the first and second stitch at the edge of the piece and works best when the first stitch is a selvage stitch.

To work this seam, thread a tapestry needle with matching yarn. Insert the needle into one corner of work from back to front, just above the cast-on stitch, leaving a 3-inch tail. Take needle to edge of other piece and bring it from back to front at the corner of this piece.

Return to the first piece and insert the needle from the right to wrong side where the thread comes out of the piece. Slip the needle upward under two horizontal threads and bring the needle through to the right side.

Cross to the other side and repeat the same process "down where you came out, under two threads and up."

Continue working back and forth on the two pieces in the same manner for about an inch,

then gently pull on the thread pulling the two pieces together. (Photo A)

Photo A

Complete the seam and fasten off. Use the beginning tail to even-up the lower edge by working a figure 8 between the cast-on stitches at the corners. Insert the threaded needle from front to back under both threads of the corner cast-on stitch on the edge opposite the tail, then into the same stitch on the first edge. Pull gently until the figure 8 fills the gap. (Photo B)

Photo B

When a project is made with a textured yarn that will not pull easily through the pieces, it is recommended that a smooth yarn of the same color be used to work the seam.

Garter Stitch Seams

The "bumps" of the garter stitch selvage nestle between each other in a garter stitch seam, often producing a nearly reversible seam. This is a good seam for afghan strips and blocks of the same color. Starting as for the mattress seam, work from bump to bump, alternating sides. In this case you enter each stitch only once.

Matching Patterns

When it comes to matching stripes and other elements in a sweater design, a simple method makes things line up perfectly:

Begin the seam in the usual way.

Enter the first stitch of each new color stripe (or pattern detail) on the same side as you began the seam; i.e. the same side as your tail is hanging.

KITCHENER STITCH

This method of grafting with two needles is used for the toes of socks and invisible joins. To graft the edges together and form an unbroken line of stockinette stitch, divide all stitches evenly onto two knitting needles—one behind the other. Thread yarn into tapestry needle. Hold needles with wrong sides together and work from right to left as follows:

Step 1: Insert tapestry needle into first stitch on front needle as to purl. Draw yarn through stitch, leaving stitch on knitting needle.

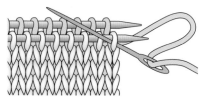

Step 2: Insert tapestry needle into the first stitch on the back needle as to purl. Draw yarn through stitch and slip stitch off knitting needle.

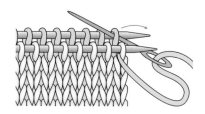

Step 3: Insert tapestry needle into the next stitch on same (back) needle as to knit, leaving stitch on knitting needle.

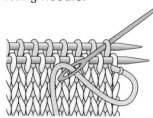

Step 4: Insert tapestry needle into the first stitch on the front needle as to knit. Draw yarn through stitch and slip stitch off knitting needle.

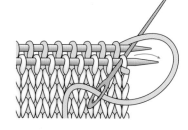

Step 5: Insert tapestry needle into the next stitch on same (front) needle as to purl. Draw yarn through stitch, leaving stitch on knitting needle.

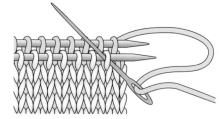

Repeat Steps 2 through 5 until one stitch is left on each needle. Then repeat Steps 2 and 4. Fasten off. Grafted stitches should be the same size as adjacent knitted stitches.

FRINGE

Cut a piece of cardboard half as long as fringe length specified in instructions plus ½ inch for trimming. Wind yarn loosely and evenly around cardboard. When cardboard is filled, cut yarn across one end. Do this several times, then begin fringing. Wind additional strands as necessary.

Single Knot Fringe

Hold specified number of strands for one knot together, fold in half. Hold project to be fringed with right side facing you. Use crochet hook to draw folded end through space or stitch indicated from right to wrong side.

Pull loose ends through folded section.

Draw knot up firmly. Space knots as indicated in pattern instructions.

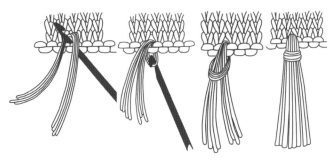

Single Knot Fringe

KNITTING WITH BEADS

Threading beads onto yarn is the most common way to knit with beads.

Step 1: Before beginning to knit, thread half of the beads onto your skein of yarn using a bead threader. As you work, unwind a small quantity of yarn, each time sliding the beads towards the ball until needed. Pass the yarn through the loop of the threader and pick up beads with the working end of the needle.

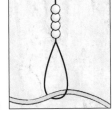

Step 2: Slide the beads over the loop and onto the yarn.

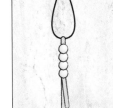

FELTING INSTRUCTIONS
The Felt Formula

Felting is not a precise science. Wool felts when exposed to water, heat and agitation, but each element is hard to control precisely. As a result, each individual project may vary in the way it felts.

Felting can be done in the sink, but washing machines get the job done more quickly. Each washing machine is different, and the rate at which specific machines felt a piece will vary. So, be sure to follow the specific felting instructions of the piece you are making, and check your piece several times during the felting process to make sure you are getting the desired results.

The felting process releases fibers which can clog your washing machine. Therefore, you may want to place items in a zippered pillowcase before putting them in the washing machine. Also, adding other laundry, such as jeans, when felting will increase the amount of agitation and speed up the process. Be careful not to use items that shed fibers of their own, such as towels.

Felting Facts

Felting a knit or crochet piece makes it shrink. Therefore, the piece you knit must start out much larger than the finished felted size will be. Shrinkage varies since there are so many factors that affect it. These variables include water temperature, the hardness of the water, how much (and how long) the piece is agitated, the amount and type of soap used, yarn brand, fiber content and color.

You can control how much your piece felts by watching it closely. Check your piece after about 10 minutes to see how quickly it is felting. Look at the stitch definition and size to determine if the piece has been felted enough.

How to Felt

Place items to be felted in the washing machine along with one tablespoon of dish detergent and a pair of jeans or other laundry. (Remember, do not felt projects with other clothing that release their own fibers.) Set washing machine on smallest load and use hot water. Start machine and check progress after ten minutes. Check progress more frequently after piece starts to felt. Reset the machine if needed to continue the agitation cycle. Do not allow machine to go to spin cycle; rapid spinning can cause creases in the felted fabric that may be very difficult to get out later. As the piece becomes more felted, you may need to pull it into shape.

When the piece has felted to the desired size, rinse it by hand in warm water. Remove the excess water either by rolling in a towel and squeezing.

Block the piece into shape, and let air dry. Do not dry in clothes dryer. For pieces that need to conform to a particular shape (such as a hat or purse), stuff the piece with a towel to help it hold its shape while drying. Felted items are very strong, so don't be afraid to push and pull it into the desired shape. It may take several hours or several days for the pieces to dry completely.

After the piece is completely dry, excess fuzziness can be trimmed with scissors if a smoother surface is desired, or the piece can be brushed for a fuzzier appearance.

3-NEEDLE BIND-OFF

Use this technique for seaming two edges together, such as when joining a shoulder seam. Hold the live edge stitches on two separate needles with right sides together.

With a third needle, knit together a stitch from the front needle with one from the back.

Repeat, knitting a stitch from the front needle with one from the back needle once more.

Slip the first stitch over the second.

Repeat knitting, a front and back pair of stitches together, then bind one pair off.

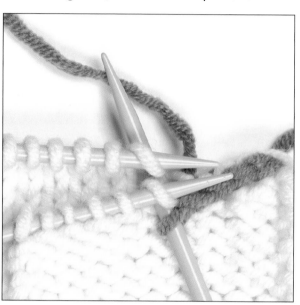

EMBROIDERY STITCHES

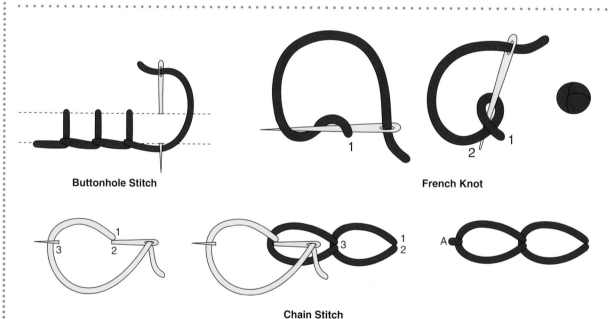

Buttonhole Stitch

French Knot

Chain Stitch

KNITTING BASICS

CAST ON

Leaving an end about an inch long for each stitch to be cast on, make a slip knot on the right needle.

Place the thumb and index finger of your left hand between the yarn ends with the long yarn end over your thumb, and the strand from the skein over your index finger. Close your other fingers over the strands to hold them against your palm. Spread your thumb and index fingers apart and draw the yarn into a "V."

Place the needle in front of the strand around your thumb and bring it underneath this strand. Carry the needle over and under the strand on your index finger.

Draw through loop on thumb.

Drop the loop from your thumb and draw up the strand to form a stitch on the needle.

Repeat until you have cast on the number of stitches indicated in the pattern. Remember to count the beginning slip knot as a stitch.

CABLE CAST-ON

This type of cast on is used when adding stitches in the middle or at the end of a row.

Make a slip knot on the left needle. Knit a stitch in this knot and place it on the left needle. Insert the right needle between the last two stitches on the left needle. Knit a stitch and place it on the left needle. Repeat for each stitch needed.

KNIT (K)

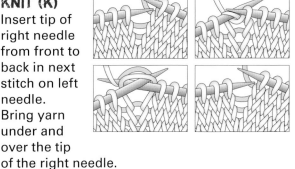

Insert tip of right needle from front to back in next stitch on left needle.

Bring yarn under and over the tip of the right needle.

Pull yarn loop through the stitch with right needle point.

Slide the stitch off the left needle. The new stitch is on the right needle.

PURL (P)

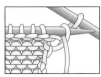

With yarn in front, insert tip of right needle from back to front through next stitch on the left needle. Bring yarn around the right needle counterclockwise. With right needle, draw yarn back through the stitch.

Slide the stitch off the left needle. The new stitch is on the right needle.

BIND-OFF

Binding off (knit)

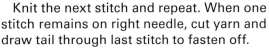

Knit first two stitches on left needle. Insert tip of left needle into first stitch worked on right needle and pull it over the second stitch and completely off the needle.

Knit the next stitch and repeat. When one stitch remains on right needle, cut yarn and draw tail through last stitch to fasten off.

Binding off (purl)

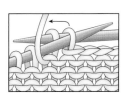

Purl first two stitches on left needle. Insert tip of left needle into first stitch worked on right needle and pull it over the second stitch and completely off the needle.

Purl the next stitch and repeat. When one stitch remains on right needle, cut yarn and draw tail through last stitch to fasten off.

INCREASE (INC)
Two stitches in one stitch
Increase (knit)

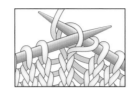

Knit the next stitch in the usual manner, but don't remove the stitch from the left needle. Place right needle behind left needle and knit again into the back of the same stitch. Slip original stitch off left needle.

Increase (purl)

Purl the next stitch in the usual manner, but don't remove the stitch from the left needle. Place right needle behind left needle and purl again into the back of the same stitch. Slip original stitch off left needle.

INVISIBLE INCREASE (M1)
There are several ways to make or increase one stitch.

Make 1 with Left Twist (M1L)

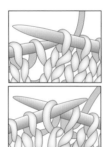

Insert left needle from front to back under the horizontal loop between the last stitch worked and next stitch on left needle.

With right needle, knit into the back of this loop.

To make this increase on the purl side, insert left needle in same manner and purl into the back of the loop.

Make 1 with Right Twist (M1R)

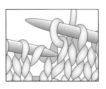

Insert left needle from back to front under the horizontal loop between the last stitch worked and next stitch on left needle.

With right needle, knit into the front of this loop.

To make this increase on the purl side, insert left needle in same manner and purl into

the front of the loop.

Make 1 with Backward Loop over the right needle

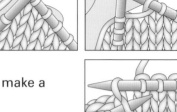

With your thumb, make a loop over the right needle.
Slip the loop from your thumb onto the needle and pull to tighten.

Make 1 in top of stitch below

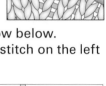

Insert tip of right needle into the stitch on left needle one row below.

Knit this stitch, then knit the stitch on the left needle.

DECREASE (DEC)
Knit 2 together (k2tog)

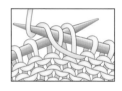

Put tip of right needle through next two stitches on left needle as to knit. Knit these two stitches as one.

Purl 2 together (p2tog)

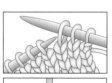

Put tip of right needle through next two stitches on left needle as to purl. Purl these two stitches as one.

SLIP, SLIP, KNIT (SSK)

Slip next two stitches, one at a time, as to knit from left needle to right needle.

Insert left needle in front of both stitches and work off needle together.

SLIP, SLIP, PURL (SSP)

Slip next two stitches, one at a time, as to knit from left needle to right needle. Slip these stitches back onto left needle keeping them twisted. Purl these two stitches together through back loops.

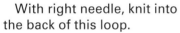

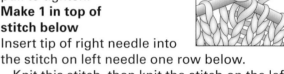

CROCHET BASICS

Some knit items are finished with a crochet trim or edging. Below are some abbreviations used in crochet and a review of some basic crochet stitches.

CROCHET ABBREVIATIONS

ch   chain stitch
dc   double crochet
hdc   half double crochet
lp(s)   loop(s)
sc   single crochet
sl st   slip stitch
yo   yarn over

CHAIN STITCH (CH)

Begin by making a slip knot on the hook. Bring the yarn over the hook from back to front and draw through the loop on the hook.

For each additional chain stitch, bring the yarn over the hook from back to front and draw through the loop on the hook.

SINGLE CROCHET (SC)

Insert the hook in the second chain through the center of the V. Bring the yarn over the hook from back to front.

Draw the yarn through the chain stitch and onto the hook.

Again bring yarn over the hook from back to front and draw it through both loops on hook.

For additional rows of single crochet, insert the hook under both loops of the previous stitch instead of through the center of the V as when working into the chain stitch.

REVERSE SINGLE CROCHET (REVERSE SC)

Working in opposite direction from single crochet, insert hook under both loops of the next stitch to the right.

Bring yarn over hook from back to front and draw through both loops on hook.

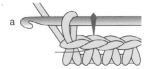

HALF-DOUBLE CROCHET (HDC)

Bring yarn over hook from back to front, insert hook in indicated chain stitch.

Draw yarn through the chain stitch and onto the hook.

Bring yarn over the hook from back to front and draw it through all three loops on the hook in one motion.

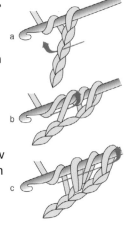

DOUBLE CROCHET (DC)

Yo, insert hook in st, yo, pull through st, (yo, pull through 2 lps) 2 times.

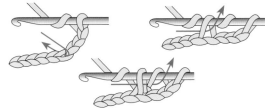

SLIP STITCH (SL ST)

Insert hook under both loops of the stitch, bring yarn over the hook from back to front and draw it through the stitch and the loop on the hook.

PICOT

Picots can be made in a variety of ways so refer to pattern for specific instructions.

Chain required number of stitches. Insert hook at base of chain stitches and through back loop of stitch, complete as indicated in pattern.

TAKE & MAKE JOURNAL

Never forget where you left off in a pattern with this template page. You can copy and carry it while you're on the road, keeping track as you go!

Date Started: _____ **This Project Was Made For:** _____

Travel Tips I Found Useful: _____

_____

Project Name & Page Number(s): _____

PROJECT ORGANIZER

Yarn Brand/Name	Color(s) & Dye Lot	Gauge (stitches x rows= 4 inches)
Number of Skeins/Balls Used	**Needle(s)**	**Notions**

Pattern repeat info: multiple of: _____ + _____ stitches.

Additional pattern repeat notes:

_____

Use the spaces below to keep track of each section you're working on. For example, if you're working on the Front of a sweater, list specific notes about that section's progress. When done, check it off and move on to the next section.

PAGE/SECTION NOTES

☐

☐

☐

☐

☐

☐

☐

☐

☐

☐

☐

☐

☐

Memorable Travel Notes: _____

_____

_____

YARN & BAG RESOURCES

Many of the yarns and bags presented in this book are available in your local yarn shop. If you should have any problems purchasing them in your area, the list below will serve as a helpful resource.

YARN

ORNAGHI FILATI YARNS
Dist. by Aurora Yarns
P.O. Box 3068
Moss Beach, CA 94038
(650) 728-2730
www.aurorayarns.net

BERROCO INC.
P.O. Box 367
14 Elmdale Road
Uxbridge, MA 01569-0367
(508) 278-2527
www.berroco.com

CARON INTERNATIONAL
Customer Service
P.O. Box 222
Washington, NC 27889
www.caron.com
www.shopcaron.com
www.naturallycaron.com

CASCADE YARNS
1224 Andover Park East
Seattle, WA 98188
(206) 574-0440
www.cascadeyarns.com

CLASSIC ELITE YARNS INC.
122 Western Ave.
Lowell, MA 01851-1434
(978) 453-2837
www.classiceliteyarns.com

COATS & CLARK
(Moda Dea)
P.O. Box 12229
Greenville, SC 29612-0229
(800) 648-1479
www.coatsandclark.com
www.modadea.com

CRYSTAL PALACE YARNS
160 23rd St.
Richmond, CA 94804
(510) 237-9988
www.straw.com

REYNOLDS
Dist. by JCA, Inc.
35 Scales Lane
Townsend, MA 01469
(978) 597-8794
www.jcacrafts.com

KNIT ONE, CROCHET TOO INC.
91 Tandberg Trail, Unit 6
Windham, ME 04062
(207) 892-9625
www.knitonecrochettoo.com

MISSION FALLS
5333 Casgrain #1204
Montreal, Quebec
H2T 1X3 Canada
(877) 244-1204
www.missionfalls.com

NASHUA HANDKNITS
Dist. by Westminster Fibers Inc.
165 Ledge St.
Nashua, NH 03060
(800) 445-9276
www.nashuaknits.com
www.westminsterfibers.com

PLYMOUTH YARN COMPANY INC.
500 Lafayette St.
Bristol, PA 19007
(215) 788-0459
www.plymouthyarn.com

PRISM ARTS INC.
2595 30th Ave. North
St. Petersburg, FL 33713
(727) 321-1905
www.prismyarn.com

ROWAN
Dist. by Westminster Fibers Inc.
165 Ledge St.
Nashua, NH 03060
(800) 445-9276
www.knitrowan.com
www.westminsterfibers.com

SCHACHENMAYR
Dist. by Westminster Fibers Inc.
165 Ledge St.
Nashua, NH 03060
(800) 445-9276
www.schachenmayr.us
www.westminsterfibers.com

SCHAEFER YARN COMPANY LTD.
3514 Kelly's Corners Road
Interlaken, NY 14847
(607) 532-9452
www.schaeferyarn.com

SPINRITE LP
(Lily Sugar n' Cream, Patons)
320 Livingstone Ave. S.
Listowel, ON
N4W 3H3 Canada
(888) 368-8401
www.spinriteyarns.com
www.sugarncream.com
www.patonsyarns.com

TAHKI STACY CHARLES INC.
70-30 80th St. Building 36
Ridgewood, NY 11385
(800) 338-YARN (9276)
www.tahkistacycharles.com

TRENDSETTER YARNS
16745 Saticoy St. Suite #101
Van Nuys, CA 91406
(800) 446-2425
www.trendsetteryarns.com

BAGS

ATENTI
2336 Mountain Ave.
La Crescenta, CA 91214
(818) 248 8459
www.atenti.net
Disks Satchel, Page 38
Kiss Me Doctor Bag,
    Page 140

DELLA Q
2637 2nd Ave. N.
Seattle, WA 98109
(877) 733-5527
www.dellaq.com
Eden Cotton Project Bag,
    Page 1.
Molly, Page 6
Rosemary, Page 176

LANTERN MOON
7911 N.E. 33rd Drive,
    Suite 140
Portland, OR 97211
(800) 530-4170
www.lanternmoon.com
Calypso, Cover.
Garden Taffeta in silver,
    Page 173.
Libby, Page 106 and
    Back Cover.

NAMASTE, INC.
9025 Eton Ave. Suite B
Canoga Park, CA 91304
(818) 717-9134
www.namasteneedles.com
Needle Binder, Page 66.

PHOTO INDEX

ACCENT ACCESSORIES

Uptown Chic Satchel, 7

Little Miss Hat & Purse, 10

Kathmandu Cravat, 14

Day at the Met Mitered Wrap, 16

Country Roads Scarf, 19

Simply Stripes Scarf, 22

City Girl Scarf, 24

Kaleidoscope Market Bag, 26

Harlequin Socks, 29

Traveling Lace Beaded Shawl, 32

Gossamer Capelet, 35

WANDERING WEARABLES

Dual Texture Tunic, 39

European Tour Set, 42

Casual Cotton T-Shirt, 48

Sleek & Stylish Sleeveless Top, 52

Take It On the Road Tank, 55

"It's a Wrap" Cabled Shrug, 58

Outback Basket Weave Pullover, 62

FOR THE LITTLE ONES

Roundabout Ruffled Top, 67

Little Princess Dress Up Set, 70

Bodacious Bobble Hat, 74

Lacy A-Line Baby Dress, 76

Baby Dearest, 80

Saucy Stripes Pullover, 85

Cozy Hooded Sleeping Sack, 88

Happy Baby Blankie, 92

A-Dorable A-Line Ruffled Jumper, 95

Little Sailor Cami &
Soaker Pants, 98

Tonal Triangles Kids'
Pullover, 102

GIFTY THINGS

Cable Sampler
Baby Blocks, 107

Nautical Stripes
Onesie & Sunhat, 110

Cute as a Button
Baby Set, 114

Day at the Beach Flip-
Flops & Bracelet, 118

Andrea Beaded Cuffs,
121

Easy as 1-2-3
Braided Belt, 124

Orient Express
Eye Pillow, 126

Fanciful Felted Purse,
128

Chico's Sweater, 131

Frilly Prilly Poncho, 134

Luxurious Lace Collar,
137

HOME
ADORNMENTS

Rustic Basket Weave
Table Runner, 141

Pretty Pastels Lap
Blanket, 144

Laced-Up Cables
Afghan, 147

Spiraled I-Cord
Seat Cover, 150

Knit, Then Weave,
Place Mats, 152

Earth Tones Afghan, 155

Luxembourg Lace
Place Mats, 158

Bamboo Bath Mat, 160

SPECIAL THANKS

This book would not be a success without the talents of the following designers. We would like to thank them for contributing their imaginative designs to help make this book possible.